Beyond the Eye Roll

Navigating the Emotional World of Teens

By: Dr. Ben Smith

Overview

Children go through a spectrum of emotions, ranging from joy and excitement to sadness and anger. This book serves as your roadmap for guiding your child through these emotional highs and lows. Filled with interactive activities and discussion prompts, it enables you to connect with your child more deeply, grasp their feelings, and cultivate a strong, supportive relationship. Whether you are commemorating joyful milestones or navigating challenging situations, you will discover techniques and resources to enhance your child's emotional well-being and foster a loving family atmosphere. Additionally, if you're leveraging technology to understand your child's emotions, this book provides further methods to transform those insights into opportunities for deepening connection and growth.

Table of Contents

Happy:

When parents notice their child radiating joy and a zest for life, it's a wonderful opportunity to nurture that happiness and help it flourish. The following activities and conversations aim to celebrate and support a child's positive emotions while also deepening the connection between parent and child and fostering a lifelong appreciation for happiness:

Shared Activities

Engaging in activities a child enjoys is a powerful way to strengthen the familial bond and create lasting memories. This could involve participating in a wide range of activities that cater to the child's interests, such as playing a favorite board game, embarking on a bike ride through the neighborhood, or dedicating time to a shared hobby. These activities provide a fun and enjoyable way to spend time together and allow parents to show genuine interest in their child's passions and preferences. The joy and laughter experienced during these moments can foster a deep sense of connection and belonging, making the child feel valued and understood. This mutual enjoyment is critical to building a strong and enduring relationship.

Celebration Meal

Preparing a special meal together or visiting a favorite restaurant can be a meaningful way to celebrate a child's happiness and communicate that their feelings are valued. This shared culinary experience, whether crafting a family recipe at home or choosing a beloved dish at a restaurant, serves as a tangible expression of love and appreciation. Engaging in the process of meal preparation allows for collaboration and teamwork, providing a sense of achievement and joy when the meal is finally ready to be enjoyed together. It's an opportunity for parents to teach cooking skills or share stories associated with certain foods, creating a rich tapestry of family history and culture. Meanwhile, dining out at a favorite restaurant can turn an ordinary day into a special occasion, making the child feel celebrated and significant. These moments around the dining table become milestones in the child's emotional journey, reinforcing their sense of security and belonging.

Gratitude Journaling

Allocating time to discuss and reflect on the aspects of the day or week for which each family member is grateful is a valuable practice that fosters a positive outlook and reinforces family bonds. This deliberate focus on gratitude shifts attention away from daily frustrations and challenges, highlighting instead the moments of joy, accomplishment, and even simple pleasures. By sharing these reflections among family members, everyone is encouraged to recognize and appreciate the positive aspects of their lives, often noticing things they might have otherwise taken for granted.

Documenting these moments of gratitude in a shared journal serves as a record of positive memories and a tool for building a habit of appreciation and positivity. This practice can lead to deeper conversations about individual experiences and feelings, promoting empathy and understanding within the family.

Storytelling

Sharing stories within the family about times when each member felt particularly happy or overcame obstacles to achieve happiness is a profound way to connect on a deeper level. These narratives offer a window into the individual's inner world, revealing the strengths, vulnerabilities, and values that guide them. When family members open up about their happiest moments or recount how they navigated challenges to find joy, it encourages a culture of openness and mutual respect. This exchange of personal experiences highlights the diverse ways in which happiness can be experienced and pursued and showcases each family member's resilience and determination.

11

Through these stories, lessons of courage, perseverance, and optimism are passed down, inspiring others in the family to face their own challenges with hope and strength.

Planning a Future Activity

Planning a future outing or activity together that resonates with a child's interests is a powerful way to show them that their happiness and passions are valued. This collaborative planning process gives the child a sense of agency and involvement and reinforces the message that their preferences matter profoundly to their parents. By focusing on an event or activity that excites the child, parents can significantly boost their child's morale and enthusiasm, offering them something eagerly anticipated in the future. This anticipation of positive experiences can be incredibly motivating and uplifting for a child, especially during times that might be challenging or mundane. Moreover, planning fosters a stronger bond and mutual respect, as it involves open communication, shared decision-making, and a mutual looking forward to shared experiences. Such activities enrich the child's life with joyful experiences and cement a family dynamic where each member's individuality and happiness are central priorities.

Emotional Intelligence Conversations

Discussing the emotions involved in happiness, such as joy, contentment, and satisfaction, and emphasizing the importance of recognizing and appreciating these positive feelings play a crucial role in enhancing emotional intelligence within the family. By having open conversations about what happiness feels like, what might trigger it, and how to cultivate it, family members can develop a deeper understanding of their emotional landscapes and those of others. This kind of dialogue encourages individuals to pay closer attention to their emotional states, fostering an environment where positive feelings are sought after, cherished, and shared. Such discussions can lead to a greater capacity for empathy as family members learn to recognize and value the happiness in others as much as in themselves. Moreover, by highlighting the importance of acknowledging and savoring moments of happiness, these conversations can teach resilience, showing that there are always glimmers of joy, even in challenging times. Ultimately, engaging in discussions about the nature of happiness and the complexity of emotions associated with it can strengthen the emotional bonds between family members, creating a more empathetic, understanding, and emotionally intelligent family dynamic.

Creative Projects

Engaging in a creative project together, like painting, crafting, or building something, offers a unique opportunity for family members to express themselves individually while working towards a common goal. This collaborative creativity fosters a sense of expressive freedom and cultivates an environment where each person's ideas and contributions are valued and celebrated. As the project progresses, the shared experience of creating something from nothing becomes a source of pride and accomplishment for everyone involved. This co-creation process can significantly strengthen familial bonds, requiring communication, cooperation, and mutual support. Moreover, the finished project serves as a tangible reminder of what can be achieved together, reinforcing the sense of unity and shared identity within the family. Through such creative endeavors, family members learn more about each other's creative abilities and preferences and develop a deeper appreciation for the power of collaboration and the joy of shared success.

Nature Walk

Taking a walk in a natural setting offers a serene backdrop for parents and children to explore and discuss the inherent beauty of the natural world and its profound connection to feelings of happiness. This simple yet impactful activity encourages mindfulness as both parent and child become more attuned to the present moment, noticing the subtle details of the environment around them—the texture of tree bark, the melody of bird songs, or the dance of leaves in the wind. Engaging in conversations about how these elements of nature evoke a sense of wonder and contentment can deepen the appreciation for the world's beauty and its effects on our well-being. This shared experience fosters a greater connection to nature and strengthens the emotional bond between parent and child. It provides a valuable lesson in finding joy and tranquility in life's simple pleasures and demonstrates the importance of slowing down and being present. Such activities remind us of the interconnectedness of all living things and the positive impact nature can have on our mental and emotional states, enhancing the parent-child relationship through shared insights and experiences of mindfulness and happiness.

Watch a Movie Together

Choosing to watch a feel-good movie or a child's favorite film together provides an excellent opportunity for family bonding and can serve as a catalyst for meaningful conversations. This shared activity allows for relaxation and enjoyment and opens the door to discussing the themes, characters, and emotions portrayed in the film. Whether the movie highlights themes of friendship, courage, or overcoming challenges, it can prompt discussions about how these themes relate to personal experiences or aspirations. As family members share their perspectives on the movie's emotional journey, it encourages empathy and understanding, allowing each person to express their feelings and thoughts in a safe and supportive environment. Moreover, discussing the characters' decisions, obstacles, and triumphs can lead to deeper conversations about values, ethics, and personal growth. This process not only enhances emotional intelligence by helping children articulate their feelings and understand those of others but also strengthens the parent-child connection through shared experiences and insights. Watching and discussing movies together, especially those that resonate emotionally, can be a valuable tool for parents to explore and navigate the complexities of emotions with their children, fostering a deeper connection and mutual understanding.

Feedback and Appreciation

Providing positive feedback and expressing appreciation for a child's qualities and achievements plays a critical role in nurturing their self-esteem and happiness. When parents take the time to recognize and celebrate their child's efforts, talents, and accomplishments, it sends a powerful message of validation and support. This recognition can be as simple as praising their persistence in solving a complex puzzle, acknowledging their kindness in sharing with a friend or celebrating their bravery in trying something new. Parents help their children understand and appreciate their strengths and capabilities by focusing on specific qualities and achievements. Such positive reinforcement validates the child's feelings, making them feel seen and heard, and also boosts their self-esteem, encouraging a positive self-image. Over time, this practice of acknowledgment and appreciation builds confidence in the child, empowering them to pursue their interests and face challenges with resilience. Moreover, it strengthens the bond between parent and child, as the child feels genuinely supported and valued for who they are. This positive feedback and appreciation environment is essential for fostering a child's sense of worth and happiness, laying the groundwork for their emotional and psychological development.

These activities and conversations not only celebrate the child's current state of happiness but also reinforce the bond between the parent and child, creating a supportive and understanding environment that values emotional expression and mutual enjoyment.

Confident:

When parents receive a notification indicating their child is feeling confident, it provides a perfect opportunity to engage in activities and conversations that not only celebrate this positive state but also reinforce the child's self-esteem and the parent-child bond. Here are several ideas for activities and conversations designed to support and enhance the relationship between parents and their children in moments of confidence:

Acknowledge and Discuss

Initiating a conversation by recognizing and acknowledging a child's confidence is a significant first step in nurturing their self-awareness and boosting their self-esteem. By pointing out moments when the child demonstrated confidence, parents can open up a meaningful dialogue about the feelings and actions that led to those moments. Asking open-ended questions about how they achieved such a state of confidence, what strategies they used, and how it made them feel allows the child to reflect on their experiences and emotions. This reflective process validates their feelings, making them feel seen and understood, and promotes a deeper level of self-awareness. It encourages children to recognize their strengths and capabilities, understand the importance of their achievements, and appreciate the effort it took to reach that point of confidence. Such conversations can also provide insights into the child's thought processes and decision-making skills, offering further opportunities for parents to support and encourage their child's development. Engaging in discussions about confidence in this way strengthens the parent-child relationship, as it demonstrates a genuine interest in the child's internal world and supports their emotional growth.

Set New Challenges

Capitalizing on a moment of confidence by setting new, slightly challenging goals together is a strategic way to develop a child's self-assurance and resilience further. By choosing goals that stretch their abilities—such as mastering a new skill, auditioning for a team, or undertaking a complex project—parents can help their children build on their current state of confidence. This approach reinforces their belief in the child's capabilities and demonstrates to the child that they are supported in their endeavors to grow and excel. Working towards and achieving these new goals can provide valuable lessons in perseverance, problem-solving, and the satisfaction of overcoming obstacles. Moreover, setting these challenges together ensures that the child feels guided and encouraged, knowing they have a supportive ally in their parent. This collaborative goal-setting nurtures the child's budding confidence and strengthens the bond between parent and child as they navigate and celebrate these new achievements together. It's a powerful way to show faith in the child's potential and to motivate them to reach new heights, fostering a cycle of positive growth and self-belief.

Create a Confidence Board

Creating a visual representation of what boosts the child's confidence is a dynamic and engaging project that constantly reminds them of their strengths, achievements, and the compliments they have received. This could be a confidence board, collage, or even a digital slideshow, incorporating pictures, quotes, awards, and any tokens of personal milestones or moments of pride. Through the process of selecting and assembling these elements, the child is encouraged to reflect on their accomplishments and the qualities that contribute to their sense of confidence. This activity makes for a fun and creative bonding experience and reinforces the child's self-esteem by visually celebrating their successes and positive attributes. The finished project, placed in a prominent location, is a powerful, everyday reminder of the child's capabilities and worth. It bolsters their confidence, especially in moments of doubt or challenge, reminding them of their unique talents and the support they have from their family. Such a project highlights the importance of recognizing and cherishing one's strengths, fostering a positive self-image and a resilient spirit in the child.

Share Stories of Resilience

Sharing personal experiences or the stories of famous individuals who have exemplified confidence and resilience is a powerful tool for teaching and inspiring children. Parents can vividly illustrate the critical role of confidence in overcoming life's hurdles by narrating tales of personal triumphs over adversity or recounting the journeys of well-known figures who have faced significant challenges with courage. These stories, whether about a family member's perseverance through difficult times or a historical figure's unwavering belief in their cause despite overwhelming odds, help convey the message that obstacles and setbacks are integral to any journey toward success. Discussing how confidence and resilience were pivotal in these narratives provides children with relatable and aspirational examples and fosters a deeper emotional connection. It emphasizes to the child that they are not alone in facing challenges and that they can also navigate difficult situations with confidence and perseverance. This approach inspires children to cultivate their resilience and confidence and strengthens the bond between parent and child, as it is built on shared stories of triumph and perseverance.

Explore New Interests Together

Taking the initiative to explore new activities or hobbies with your child is a wonderful way to demonstrate support for their interests and show your willingness to step outside your comfort zone, mirroring their openness to new experiences. This shared venture into unfamiliar territory can be an exciting and enriching experience for both parent and child, whether it's learning a new language, trying out a craft, or engaging in a sport neither has attempted before. Such activities provide valuable learning opportunities and foster a sense of adventure and curiosity. By actively participating in these new hobbies together, parents send a powerful message of encouragement, showing their children that pursuing interests passionately and fearlessly is valuable. This approach helps to strengthen the bond between parent and child as they navigate the challenges and joys of learning something new side by side. It creates a shared history of unique experiences and memories, reinforcing the idea that stepping into the unknown can be a positive and rewarding journey when done together.

Celebrate Achievements

Celebrating a child's confidence and achievements is crucial in reinforcing positive behavior and fostering a supportive family environment. Recognizing these milestones, no matter how small, with a family celebration or a special outing highlights the importance of their accomplishments and boosts the child's self-esteem. It signals to the child that their efforts are seen, valued, and worthy of recognition. Whether it's a simple family dinner where the child's achievements are the toast of the evening or a special day out doing something they love, these celebrations serve as tangible rewards that encourage the continuation of confident behavior. Such acknowledgment creates a positive feedback loop, motivating the child to embrace challenges, knowing their achievements will be celebrated confidently. This approach reinforces the desired behaviors and strengthens family bonds, as these celebrations become cherished memories that underscore the family's commitment to supporting one another's growth and happiness.

Develop a Growth Mindset

Discussing the importance of a growth mindset can significantly impact how a child perceives challenges and their ability to develop confidence. By explaining that confidence is not a fixed trait but rather something that can be cultivated through effort, learning, and perseverance, parents can encourage their children to embrace challenges as opportunities for growth. This perspective helps shift the child's focus from fearing failure to valuing the learning process, understanding that each effort to overcome obstacles can increase their self-assurance and resilience. Emphasizing that every challenge is a chance to stretch their abilities and boost their confidence reinforces the idea that growth and learning are continuous processes.

Encouraging this mindset in children prepares them to tackle future challenges with a positive outlook and instills in them the belief that their actions and dedication can lead to significant personal development. This approach nurtures a resilient spirit, empowering children to view setbacks not as insurmountable barriers but as stepping stones toward becoming more confident and capable individuals.

Volunteer Together

Engaging in volunteer work together with your child, especially in areas that match their interests and strengths, offers a multifaceted learning experience that extends beyond the act of giving back. It is a practical demonstration of how individual contributions can significantly impact the community. This shared activity reinforces the value of selflessness and community service and showcases how confidence plays a pivotal role in making a positive impact. As children apply their skills and interests in a real-world context, they witness firsthand the effects of their efforts, whether it's through improving the environment, aiding those in need, or contributing to a cause they care about. This experience can boost their confidence as they see the tangible outcomes of their actions, reinforcing their belief in their ability to effect change. Moreover, volunteering together strengthens the parent-child bond through shared experiences rooted in empathy and compassion. It encourages a sense of responsibility and a deeper understanding of the world, inspiring confidence in personal abilities and the potential to contribute to the greater good.

Practice Positive Affirmations

Introducing the practice of positive affirmations can be a powerful tool for children to boost their confidence, especially during moments of doubt. By creating a set of personalized affirmations together, parents can help their children develop a repertoire of positive statements that reinforce their self-worth, abilities, and potential. This collaborative process allows the child to reflect on the strengths and qualities they appreciate about themselves, translating these reflections into simple, affirming statements they can repeat. For example, affirmations like "I am capable of overcoming challenges," "I believe in my abilities," or "I am worthy of love and respect" can be incredibly empowering. Repeating these affirmations, especially during challenging times, can help shift the child's focus from self-doubt to a positive self-conception, fostering resilience and a positive mindset. Moreover, this practice teaches children the importance of self-compassion and the power of words in shaping our self-perception and confidence levels. As children learn to encourage themselves through affirmations, they build a foundation of self-esteem and confidence that supports their growth and well-being.

Reflect on Growth

Dedicating time to reflect with your child on their personal growth and the challenges they've overcome is a valuable exercise in recognizing and celebrating their development. This reflection can take many forms, such as looking through old photographs, revisiting achievements, or simply sharing memories. By highlighting specific instances where the child faced difficulties and emerged stronger, parents can help their child see tangible evidence of their resilience and growing confidence. Discussing these moments encourages the child to acknowledge their progress and the hard work that went into overcoming obstacles, fostering a sense of pride and accomplishment. This process reinforces the child's self-esteem and strengthens the parent-child bond through shared memories and mutual recognition of the child's journey. It serves as a reminder that growth often comes from facing and navigating challenges and that each experience contributes to their overall development. Such reflections can inspire continued perseverance and confidence as the child faces new challenges, knowing they have a history of overcoming obstacles and growing stronger because of them.

Engaging in these activities and conversations acknowledges and celebrates the child's current confidence and provides them with tools and strategies to maintain and build upon it. It fosters an environment where the child feels supported and understood, strengthening the bond between parent and child.

Excited:

When parents receive a notification indicating their child is excited, it presents a wonderful opportunity to engage in supportive activities and conversations that share in the child's excitement and deepen the bond between parent and child. Here are several ideas for parents looking to capitalize on their child's excitement to foster a closer relationship:

Share in the Excitement

Starting with an expression of genuine excitement about what has sparked joy in your child is a powerful way to communicate your support and validate their feelings. Sharing in their excitement reinforces that their interests and achievements are important to you and strengthens your emotional connection. Whether it's a small accomplishment, a discovery, or anticipation of an upcoming event, mirroring their enthusiasm shows that you are attuned to their feelings and value what brings them happiness. This shared joy can encourage your child to open up more about their experiences and passions, knowing they have a supportive and interested audience in you. Additionally, this approach fosters a positive family atmosphere where enthusiasm and achievements are celebrated together, creating a nurturing environment that boosts the child's self-esteem and confidence. Celebrating their excitement this way lays a foundation for open communication and mutual respect, deepening the bond between parent and child.

Explore the Source of Excitement

Having an open conversation with your child about what excites them is crucial in showing that you value their interests and emotions. You demonstrate a genuine interest in their world by asking thoughtful questions about the source of their excitement, whether it be a new hobby, an upcoming event, or a personal achievement. This kind of dialogue encourages your child to share more about what matters to them, deepening your understanding of their passions and perspectives. It's an opportunity to explore their feelings and the reasons behind their enthusiasm, which can reveal more about their personality, desires, and how they engage with the world around them. Engaging in such conversations validates their feelings, making them feel seen and heard and strengthening the bond between parent and child. It sends a clear message that their interests are important and worthy of attention, fostering an environment of mutual respect and open communication. This approach helps build a strong foundation of trust and support, crucial elements for a healthy and nurturing relationship.

Plan a Related Activity

When a child's excitement centers on a specific event, hobby, or interest, planning a related activity together can significantly enhance their enthusiasm and deepen your connection. For instance, if a child eagerly anticipates a science fair, collaborating on a small experiment at home aligns with their current interest and provides a practical, hands-on way to explore and learn together. This approach demonstrates your support for their passions and willingness to actively engage in what matters to them. A home experiment could involve simple materials and questions that spark curiosity, encouraging a love for learning and discovery. This shared experience reinforces the child's interest in science and offers valuable one-on-one time, showing them that their passions are worth investing time and energy into. It's a way to build confidence in pursuing their interests while creating memorable moments that strengthen your bond. By participating in activities related to their interests, you help cultivate their enthusiasm, demonstrate your support for their endeavors, and show them that their excitement is contagious and valued.

Create a Countdown

Creating a countdown calendar with your child in anticipation of an upcoming event is a delightful activity that can significantly enhance their excitement and provide a tangible way to visualize the approach of the day. This engaging process involves marking off each day leading up to the event, turning the passage of time into a shared and enjoyable experience. Not only does this build anticipation, but it also allows for daily moments of connection between parent and child as you reflect on the decreasing number of days. To make the countdown even more special, you can personalize the calendar with decorations, stickers, or notes related to the event, adding an element of creativity and personal touch to the anticipation. This activity becomes a daily ritual that both parent and child look forward to, fostering a sense of shared excitement and making the waiting period an integral part of the event. It's a wonderful way to show your child you share in their enthusiasm and support their interests, strengthening your bond over the shared joy and anticipation for what's to come.

Prepare Together

If a child's excitement is linked to an upcoming event or competition, dedicating time to prepare together can be an excellent way to share their enthusiasm and show your unwavering support. Whether it involves practicing skills, assembling required materials, or strategizing for the event, your active involvement highlights the importance of their interests and goals. This collaborative preparation helps them feel more confident and ready and strengthens the bond between you through shared objectives and teamwork. For example, if the event is a sports competition, practicing together or discussing tactics can enhance their physical readiness and strategic understanding while providing opportunities for encouragement and bonding. Similarly, if it's a creative competition, such as a science fair or an art contest, working together to gather supplies, brainstorm ideas, or refine their project can be equally rewarding. These shared efforts underscore your commitment to their success and well-being, reinforcing the idea that their passions and achievements are valued. Moreover, this collaborative approach teaches valuable lessons in dedication, planning, and perseverance, setting a foundation for future endeavors and strengthening the supportive framework within the family dynamic.

Encourage Sharing Their Excitement

Encouraging your child to share their excitement with other family members or friends can be valuable in expressing their feelings and spreading joy. Suggesting that they make a small presentation at home or initiate a phone call to grandparents allows them to articulate what they are looking forward to and enhances their communication skills. This sharing can be empowering and uplifting, as it validates their emotions and gives them a platform to express themselves. For the child, the experience of telling others about their anticipation or achievements and receiving positive feedback and support can significantly boost their confidence and self-esteem. Moreover, this excitement sharing can strengthen familial bonds and friendships, as joy is contagious and can bring people closer together. It encourages a culture of openness and mutual support within the family, where everyone takes an interest in and celebrates each other's happiness and milestones. This practice of expressing and sharing joy enriches the child's social and emotional development and fosters a sense of community and belonging among loved ones.

Document the Excitement

Collaborating with your child to create a journal entry, video, or photo album dedicated to what excites them is an enriching activity that captures the essence of the moment while fostering their creative expression. This project allows them to explore and articulate their feelings in a tangible form through written words, visual storytelling, or photography. For instance, journaling about an upcoming event or interest lets them express their anticipation and thoughts in detail while creating a video or photo album, which can capture the excitement and energy visually and dynamically. Such activities serve as a creative outlet and a lasting keepsake that they can look back on, reminding them of the things that brought them joy. Moreover, engaging in this creative process strengthens the parent-child bond, as it involves sharing ideas, collaborating, and appreciating each other's contributions to the project. It's a way to validate their feelings and interests, showing that what matters to them is worth commemorating and celebrating. This approach enriches the child's emotional and creative development and instills in them the value of documenting life's joyful moments.

Reflect on Past Excitements

Engaging in a conversation about past events that brought excitement to you and your child is a wonderful way to revisit shared joyful experiences and further strengthen your bond. Reflecting on these moments together, whether holiday celebrations, family vacations, achievements, or simple everyday joys, reminds you of the happiness you've shared.

This reflection rekindles those positive feelings and reinforces the sense of connection and shared history between you. It's an opportunity to highlight the importance of family, togetherness, and the joy of shared experiences. Moreover, reminiscing about past excitements can offer valuable perspectives on how you've grown together and the many experiences you've enjoyed as a unit. It reassures your child that their life is filled with moments of happiness and that they have a constant companion in you to share in these experiences. Such conversations can inspire a sense of gratitude and anticipation for future adventures together, ensuring that your child recognizes the value of family bonds and the collective memories you continue to build.

Learn More Together

When your child's excitement stems from learning something new or delving into a hobby, embracing this opportunity to explore the topic together can be a rewarding experience. Dedicating time to research or watch documentaries related to their interest shows your support for their curiosity and enhances your knowledge and understanding. This joint learning endeavor can serve as an educational adventure where both parent and child discover new facts, ideas, and perspectives. It transforms the learning process into a shared journey, making it more engaging and meaningful. Additionally, this quality time spent together in pursuit of knowledge deepens your bond, as it involves cooperation, discussion, and mutual excitement about the discoveries made along the way. Whether the topic is a scientific phenomenon, a historical event, or a craft technique, diving into it together can open up new avenues for conversation and connection, fostering a culture of lifelong learning and curiosity within the family. This approach supports your child's interests and educational development and strengthens the familial relationship through shared experiences and the joy of learning together.

Express Confidence and Encouragement

Reinforcing your child's excitement with words of encouragement and expressing confidence in their abilities significantly impacts their self-esteem and the strength of your relationship. When you vocalize your belief in their capabilities, especially in areas that excite them, it validates their interests and boosts their confidence to pursue these passions. This support can be a powerful motivator for children, encouraging them to enthusiastically tackle new challenges and explore their interests. Hearing that you have faith in their abilities reinforces their self-worth and can inspire them to push beyond their limits, knowing they have your unwavering support. Additionally, this expression of confidence and encouragement fosters a deeper trust and connection, showing that you are genuinely invested in their happiness and growth. It communicates to your child that their passions and endeavors are important and that you are there to cheer them on every step of the way. Such supportive interactions nurture your child's development and strengthen the bond between you, creating a foundation of mutual respect and understanding that enhances your relationship.

By engaging in these activities and conversations, parents join in their child's excitement and foster an environment of shared joy, mutual respect, and deepened connections. This approach ensures children feel supported and understood, strengthening the familial bond.

Content:

When parents receive a notification indicating their child is content, it's an opportune moment to engage in activities and conversations that reinforce this positive emotional state, deepen understanding, and enhance their bond. Here are several suggestions for parents to consider:

Reflective Conversations

Initiating a conversation with your child about what makes them feel content is a meaningful way to gain insight into their inner world, including their needs, desires, and what truly brings them joy. By inquiring about the sources of their contentment, you create a space for open dialogue, encouraging them to reflect on and articulate the aspects of their life that fulfill them the most. This process deepens your understanding of your child and shows them that their feelings and well-being are important to you. Such conversations can reveal much about what your child values, whether it's quiet time spent reading, activities shared with friends, or accomplishments in personal projects. Understanding these facets of their happiness can guide you in supporting their interests and creating more opportunities for contentment in their lives. Furthermore, acknowledging and discussing these moments of contentment fosters a deeper emotional connection between you and your child, as it highlights a mutual interest in each other's happiness and well-being. This attentive and caring approach to understanding your child's sources of joy and satisfaction strengthens your bond, building a foundation of trust and open communication.

Gratitude Journaling

Starting a gratitude journal with your child offers a structured and reflective way to acknowledge and appreciate the positive aspects of your lives. By regularly recording things you both are thankful for, you cultivate an atmosphere of positivity, encouraging a shift in focus towards appreciation and away from negativity or taking things for granted. This practice nurtures a positive outlook and significantly strengthens the emotional bond between you, as it involves shared moments of reflection and gratitude. The act of writing down these grateful thoughts can be a calming and bonding activity, providing an opportunity to discuss what makes each of you feel thankful and why. It helps recognize and celebrate the simple joys and blessings, reinforcing the value of gratitude in daily life. Over time, this journal becomes a cherished record of positive memories and moments you have acknowledged and celebrated together, enhancing your connection and providing a tangible reminder of the strength and beauty of your relationship. This ongoing practice of gratitude can profoundly impact both your and your child's emotional well-being, fostering a deeper, more meaningful bond rooted in mutual appreciation and positivity.

Nature Walks

Taking a walk in nature together provides a serene backdrop for appreciating the beauty and tranquility of the natural world, fostering a sense of contentment and peace. This simple yet profound activity allows both parent and child to step away from the hustle and bustle of daily life, immersing themselves in the calming effects of nature. Walking amidst trees, along a beach, or through a park encourages mindfulness and a deeper appreciation for the environment, amplifying feelings of well-being and relaxation. In this peaceful setting, free from distractions, meaningful conversations can naturally arise, enabling a deeper connection. Discussing observations about the natural surroundings, sharing thoughts, or simply enjoying the silence can strengthen the bond between parent and child. These moments spent in nature offer a respite from everyday stresses and provide a valuable opportunity for both to reflect, connect, and nurture a shared sense of gratitude for the world around them.

Quiet Time Together

In the quiet companionship of shared activities like reading books side by side or listening to calming music, parents and children can find a profound sense of contentment and connection that transcends the need for conversation. These moments of peaceful coexistence, where the hustle of daily life fades into the background, offer a unique opportunity to strengthen bonds in silence. The simplicity of these activities fosters an atmosphere of tranquility and shared space, allowing both parent and child to enjoy each other's presence in a relaxed and comforting environment. This kind of silent togetherness can be especially meaningful, demonstrating that connection does not always require words; it can be felt by being together engaged in parallel activities that bring joy and calm. These moments of quiet companionship can deepen the emotional connection, creating a shared experience of peace and contentment that enriches the relationship.

Mindfulness Activities

Engaging in mindfulness activities together, such as meditation or deep-breathing exercises, offers a shared path to contentment while teaching valuable skills for emotional balance. These practices encourage both parent and child to focus on the present moment, cultivating peace and centeredness amidst life's inevitable stresses. By taking the time to meditate or perform deep-breathing exercises together, you model healthy coping mechanisms for your child and experience the benefits firsthand, including reduced anxiety, improved focus, and a heightened sense of well-being. This shared experience can deepen your bond as you learn to navigate and manage emotions together, fostering a supportive environment for emotional growth. These mindfulness practices can also become a cherished part of your daily routine, offering tranquility and connection in your busy lives. Engaging in these activities together demonstrates a commitment to each other's mental and emotional health, reinforcing the importance of caring for oneself and each other.

Creative Projects

Working on a creative project together, like painting, crafting, or building something, opens up a vibrant avenue for shared contentment and a deeper understanding of each other's personalities and preferences. Engaging in creative expression fosters a sense of joy and accomplishment and encourages communication and collaboration, revealing insights into each other's creative process, aesthetic preferences, and problem-solving strategies. Whether deciding on colors for a painting, choosing materials for a craft, or planning the steps to build a project, each decision and action offers a glimpse into the other's thoughts and feelings. This cooperative, creative endeavor can lead to moments of shared inspiration and innovation, enhancing the bond between parent and child through the joy of making something together. Additionally, the act of creating together serves as a tangible reminder of the time spent together, filled with learning and enjoyment. Such activities nurture a sense of contentment through creation and build a foundation of mutual respect and appreciation for each other's unique contributions and perspectives.

Cooking or Baking Together

Preparing a meal or treat together is a heartwarming activity that enhances the sense of contentment and fosters a delightful sense of accomplishment. The shared cooking or baking experience invites collaboration and creativity, turning the kitchen into a stage for mutual learning and fun. As both parent and child engage in the process of measuring, mixing, and maybe even experimenting with flavors, they create something delicious and build precious memories. Cooking together goes beyond food preparation; it becomes an opportunity for bonding, sharing stories, and laughing over mishaps. The joy found in tasting the fruits of your joint efforts can instill a deep sense of pride and happiness, reinforcing the idea that together, you can achieve delightful results. This fulfilling activity brings about contentment through the pleasure of eating and the shared journey of making the meal or treats, cementing a connection built on shared experiences and the simple joy of nourishing each other.

Sharing Stories

Sharing personal stories of contentment, alongside the challenges faced and overcome, can significantly enrich the emotional landscape between you and your child. By opening up about your own journeys, both the highs and the lows, you not only humanize yourself in your child's eyes but also offer them valuable life lessons from someone they trust and admire. Discussing moments when you felt genuinely content can inspire your child to seek and recognize their happiness. Equally, recounting the obstacles you've encountered and the strategies you employed to navigate them provides practical examples of resilience and problem-solving. This exchange of experiences fosters empathy and understanding, as it allows your child to see the world through your eyes, understanding that challenges and contentment are universal aspects of the human experience. Such conversations can deepen your emotional bond, creating a foundation of trust and open communication. It reassures your child that they are not alone in their feelings and that they have a supportive guide in you who has navigated the complexities of life and emerged with wisdom and stories to share.

Planning a Dream Activity

While finding contentment in the present moment is invaluable, planning a future activity or trip together creates a dynamic avenue for excitement and shared anticipation. This exercise is not just about the activity itself but also about engaging in a collaborative process that strengthens bonds through shared interests and dreams. Discussing potential destinations, activities, or projects offers a glimpse into each other's aspirations and preferences, fostering mutual understanding and respect. It's an opportunity to dream together, to imagine the experiences you will share, and to build excitement for what's to come. This planning process becomes a source of joy, allowing both parent and child to contribute ideas, express enthusiasm, and make decisions together. It demonstrates the value of looking forward to and preparing for future joys, highlighting that contentment can also be found in anticipation and collective dreaming. Such activities enrich the relationship with positive expectations and instill a sense of hope and excitement for the future, deepening the connection through shared goals and aspirations.

Celebrating the Small Things

Celebrating small achievements and simple joys can profoundly reinforce the idea that contentment is not just about grand accomplishments or milestones. Still, it can also be found in the everyday moments that make up the fabric of our lives. This practice of recognizing and valuing the smaller victories or pleasures—such as mastering a new skill, enjoying a beautiful sunset, or completing daily tasks—teaches that happiness and satisfaction are often found in the journey, not just the destination. Celebrating these moments together highlights the importance of gratitude for the 'little things' and strengthens the emotional bond between you and your child by sharing these joys. It creates a positive atmosphere where both of you are encouraged to notice and appreciate the abundance of daily contentment opportunities that life offers. This shared appreciation can lead to a deeper connection, as it fosters an environment of mutual support and acknowledgment of each other's contributions to shared happiness. Cultivating this habit lays the groundwork for a resilient and optimistic outlook, demonstrating that every day holds potential for joy and achievement.

These activities and conversations are designed not just to share in the child's current state of contentment but also to build upon it, fostering an environment where the child feels understood, valued, and closely connected to their parent.

Bored:

When parents are notified that their child is feeling bored, it's a great opportunity to engage in activities and conversations that alleviate the boredom and strengthen the bond between them. Here are several suggestions:

Discover New Hobbies Together

Using this time to explore new hobbies together can be a fantastic way to inject excitement and variety into your relationship with your child. Venturing into the unknown together, whether crafting creative projects, tending a garden, or learning to play a musical instrument, offers a unique blend of challenges and rewards. Engaging in a new hobby not only presents a chance to learn and grow but also provides a platform for shared experiences and memories. Discovering a new interest together encourages teamwork, patience, and mutual support as both parent and child navigate the learning curve of their chosen activity. This journey can significantly strengthen your bond, as it is built on collaboration, shared victories, and, sometimes, the fun of learning from mistakes. The excitement of trying something new together can reinvigorate your relationship, offering fresh topics for conversation and a mutual hobby that can be enjoyed for years. Moreover, these experiences can foster a spirit of adventure and openness to new experiences in your child, showing them the value of lifelong learning and the joy of exploring new interests.

Plan a Surprise Adventure

Organizing a surprise outing or adventure for your child can be an advantageous way to break from routine and inject a sense of wonder and excitement into your time together. Surprise adds an extra layer of anticipation; the outing doesn't need to be elaborate to be memorable. A simple visit to a local park, museum, or a new area in your town can transform into an adventure, sparking curiosity and providing a fresh backdrop for exploration and learning. Such experiences offer opportunities for discovery, whether encountering new wildlife, learning about history, or simply experiencing a change of scenery. Planning this adventure with your child's interests in mind shows them you are attentive to what they enjoy and committed to making special memories together. It reinforces your bond, as shared experiences are the building blocks of a strong, connected relationship. Moreover, these outings can serve as a reminder that joy and excitement can be found in exploring the world around us, encouraging a lifelong appreciation for adventure and discovery.

Create a Story or Comic Together

Working on a creative project, such as writing a story or creating a comic book with your child can be a stimulating and enriching experience beyond mere entertainment. This activity taps into the imaginative powers of both parent and child, encouraging the flow of creativity and the exchange of ideas. The process of brainstorming storylines, developing characters, and visualizing scenes not only nurtures artistic skills but also fosters critical thinking and problem-solving abilities. Collaborating on such a project provides a unique platform for teamwork, as each person contributes their strengths and learns from the other. It's an opportunity to engage in meaningful dialogue and share insights and perspectives that enhance the story or artwork. This collaborative effort strengthens the bond between parent and child, as it is built on mutual respect for ideas and the shared joy of creating something new. Furthermore, completing a creative project brings a sense of accomplishment and pride, offering tangible proof of what can be achieved through cooperation and shared vision. It's an exercise that stimulates creativity and highlights the value of sharing and working together towards a common goal.

Science Experiments at Home

Conducting simple science experiments with your child using everyday household items can transform your home into a laboratory of learning and excitement. This hands-on approach to science brings concepts to life, sparking curiosity and a love for exploration. Whether creating a baking soda and vinegar volcano, building a homemade battery, or exploring the properties of water tension, these experiments demystify scientific principles in an engaging and accessible way. Such activities provide a fun and educational way to spend time together and encourage critical thinking and problem-solving skills as children hypothesize outcomes and observe results. Moreover, these experiments can foster a sense of wonder about the natural world and inspire questions that lead to further discovery and learning. Engaging in science activities at home shows children that learning can be interactive and enjoyable and that the world around them consists of interesting phenomena waiting to be explored. This shared exploration can strengthen the bond between parent and child as you navigate the wonders of science together, fostering a lifelong interest in learning and discovery.

Cook or Bake Together

Involving your child in cooking or baking presents a delightful opportunity for quality time together, filled with learning, creativity, and the enjoyment of a meal or treat you've made as a team. This interactive experience is not just about preparing food; it's an avenue for teaching valuable life skills such as measuring, timing, and following instructions while encouraging creativity and experimentation with flavors and ingredients. Engaging your child in the kitchen fosters a sense of responsibility and contribution to the family as they take part in creating something that everyone can enjoy. It's also a chance to pass down family recipes and share stories that revolve around food, making memories and traditions that can last a lifetime. Additionally, cooking or baking together can instill a greater appreciation for homemade meals and the effort that goes into preparing them, promoting healthier eating habits. The shared success of creating a meal or treat can be incredibly satisfying, reinforcing the bond between you through the shared accomplishment and the pleasure of sharing the fruits of your labor.

Organize a Themed Movie Night

Choosing a theme and watching movies or documentaries related to it can turn an ordinary evening into a captivating and immersive experience. This activity enriches your viewing experience and sparks curiosity and learning around the chosen theme. To elevate the experience further, incorporating themed snacks or dressing up as movie characters adds a layer of fun and engagement. For instance, if you choose a theme like "underwater adventures," you could watch films related to the ocean or marine life and enjoy seafood snacks or blue-colored drinks. Dressing up as favorite characters or sea creatures can bring the theme to life, making the experience more memorable and enjoyable for everyone involved. This themed approach to movie watching encourages creativity and imagination while also providing an opportunity to explore new topics and cultures together. It's a wonderful way to spend quality time together, offering entertainment and educational value and creating lasting memories through shared laughter and discovery.

Start a Family Book Club

Selecting a book to read together as a family and organizing regular discussions about it is a meaningful way to foster a love for reading, enhance critical thinking skills, and encourage sharing perspectives. This collective reading adventure provides a chance to dive into new worlds and ideas and creates a space for engaging dialogues about the book's characters, plot, and underlying themes. Such discussions can illuminate varied interpretations and insights, enriching the reading experience for everyone involved. It offers a unique opportunity for each family member to voice their thoughts, feelings, and questions about the book, promoting an open exchange of ideas and deepening understanding of different viewpoints. This activity strengthens family bonds through shared experiences and intellectual exploration while cultivating a habit of reading and critical analysis. Moreover, it sets a foundation for lifelong learning and curiosity, showing that books can be a source of pleasure and knowledge and that discussing literature can be a rewarding way to connect with others.

Learn Together

Choosing a new subject for you and your child to learn together presents an exciting and enriching opportunity to grow and bond as a family. Whether it's embarking on the journey of learning a new language, delving into the depths of history, or exploring the vastness of astronomy, this shared learning experience can open up new horizons and perspectives. Engaging in this educational adventure strengthens your knowledge and your relationship as you navigate the challenges and joys of learning something new side by side. This process fosters mutual support, encouragement, and admiration, as each milestone achieved is a testament to your collective effort and dedication. Moreover, learning as a family encourages open dialogue, curiosity, and the sharing of ideas, making the learning process more dynamic and interactive. It demonstrates the value of lifelong learning, showing that the pursuit of knowledge is not confined to the classroom but is a continuous journey that can be embarked upon at any age and together. This approach to learning can significantly enhance the bond between parent and child, creating lasting memories and a strong foundation of shared interests and intellectual curiosity.

DIY Projects

Engaging in DIY home projects or crafts together offers a hands-on and productive way to spend quality time, whether giving a room a new look, building a birdhouse, or channeling creativity into art. These activities foster a sense of accomplishment and satisfaction and encourage teamwork, creativity, and problem-solving. Working on a project from start to finish provides tangible results that you and your child can take pride in, showcasing the fruits of your collaborative effort. It's an opportunity to learn new skills or hone existing ones, whether that involves painting, carpentry, or artistic expression. Moreover, taking on such projects can enhance the home environment, making it a more personalized and cherished space. This shared experience strengthens the bond between parent and child through mutual effort and creativity. It instills a sense of ownership and pride in your child, showing them what can be achieved through collaboration and hard work. The memories made during these projects, alongside the skills and confidence gained, contribute to a fulfilling and enriching family experience.

Physical Activity

Introducing new forms of physical activity, such as yoga, dance, or martial arts, and practicing them together can be an excellent way to inject fun into fitness while reaping numerous benefits for physical and mental health. Engaging in these activities as a family provides a shared goal of learning and improvement and offers the chance to support and motivate each other. Whether it's the calming and strengthening poses of yoga, the rhythm and expression found in dance, or the discipline and self-defense skills of martial arts, each activity brings unique benefits and challenges. Learning these new skills together fosters a sense of teamwork and camaraderie, while physical activity promotes health, flexibility, and endurance. Moreover, the mental focus and relaxation techniques inherent in these practices can help reduce stress, enhance concentration, and improve overall well-being. This shared journey into new physical endeavors strengthens the body and mind and deepens the bond between family members through shared experiences, laughter, and encouragement, making the path to fitness a joyful and united venture.

Volunteer Together

Seeking volunteering opportunities in your community to participate in together can be a profoundly fulfilling way to spend time, offering rich lessons in empathy, compassion, and community service. Helping at a local food bank, participating in environmental clean-up efforts, or assisting at an animal shelter provides tangible ways to contribute to the well-being of others and the community. Engaging in volunteer work as a family strengthens communal bonds and instills a sense of responsibility and altruism in children. It teaches them the value of giving back and shows them firsthand the positive impact their actions can have. Moreover, volunteering together allows for meaningful conversations about the needs of others and the various ways to help, fostering a deeper understanding of empathy and compassion. This shared commitment to making a difference can enhance your family's connection to each other and your community, creating lasting memories and reinforcing the importance of working together for the common good.

Plan and Prepare for Future Goals

Using time together to discuss and plan for future goals, whether short-term objectives like enhancing a particular skill or long-term ambitions such as college planning, signifies a deep investment in your child's development and aspirations. This process provides them with a clear sense of direction and purpose and reinforces your role as a supportive and guiding figure in their life. Engaging in such discussions encourages your child to think critically about their future, set achievable objectives, and strategize on the steps needed to realize their dreams. It's an opportunity to explore their interests, strengths, and potential career paths, fostering a proactive mindset toward personal growth and achievement. Moreover, planning together for the future strengthens the bond between parent and child, as it's built on mutual respect, understanding, and shared aspirations. It communicates to your child that their dreams are important and attainable and that they have your unwavering support every step. This collaborative approach to goal setting and planning can significantly boost your child's confidence and motivation, ensuring they feel prepared and excited about the possibilities.

These activities and conversations can turn moments of boredom into opportunities for learning, growth, and deeper connection, reinforcing the bond between parent and child by sharing new experiences and discoveries.

Confused:

When a parent is notified that their child feels confused, it presents a significant opportunity to engage in supportive and constructive activities and conversations. These actions can help clarify the child's confusion and strengthen the relationship between parent and child. Here are several ideas:

Open Dialogue

Initiating a calm and open conversation about their confusion or concerns with your child is vital in helping them navigate uncertainties. You emphasize the importance of understanding over quick fixes by creating a supportive environment where they feel comfortable expressing their feelings and thoughts without fear of immediate judgment or unsolicited advice. This approach allows you to fully grasp the root of their confusion, whether it pertains to academic challenges, social situations, or personal dilemmas. Listening attentively demonstrates to your child that their feelings are valid and essential, fostering a sense of trust and openness. It's an opportunity to guide them toward self-reflection and critical thinking, encouraging them to articulate their thoughts and identify precisely what is causing their confusion. This process not only aids in clarifying the issue at hand but strengthens your bond through mutual respect and communication. By prioritizing understanding and empathy over immediate solutions, you empower your child to develop problem-solving skills and resilience, showing them that navigating through confusion is a part of learning and growth.

Problem-Solving Together

After identifying the specific area of confusion, collaborating with your child to brainstorm potential solutions or strategies to gain clarity becomes a powerful exercise in empowerment and problem-solving. This collaborative approach involves them actively in finding solutions and instills a valuable lesson: confusion is a natural and normal part of the learning journey, not a barrier to it. By working together to think of different approaches or resources that could help—whether it's seeking additional information, asking for help from a teacher or mentor, or breaking the problem down into smaller, more manageable parts— you encourage your child to view challenges as solvable puzzles rather than insurmountable obstacles. This method fosters a mindset of resilience and adaptability, crucial skills for lifelong learning and personal growth. Moreover, engaging in this process strengthens the trust and communication between you and your child, as they see you not just as a guide or authority figure but as a supportive partner in their quest for understanding. It's an approach that addresses the immediate confusion and prepares them for future challenges, reinforcing the idea that with creativity, patience, and collaboration, clarity and understanding are always within reach.

Educational Activities

If your child's confusion is rooted in academic subjects, engaging in educational activities that approach the topic from various angles can be particularly effective. By introducing diversity in learning methods, such as leveraging online resources, incorporating educational games, or conducting practical experiments, you can help demystify the subject matter. This multifaceted approach caters to different learning styles, visual, auditory, kinesthetic, or a combination, making it easier for your child to grasp complex concepts. For instance, online tutorials can provide visual and auditory explanations that clarify difficult topics, while educational games make learning interactive and fun, reinforcing concepts through play. Practical experiments, especially in subjects like science or math, offer hands-on experience, bringing abstract concepts to life. These varied learning activities alleviate confusion and ignite curiosity and a love for learning, showing your child that understanding can be achieved in multiple ways. Furthermore, actively exploring these resources supports your child's educational journey, demonstrating your commitment to their success and well-being. This approach addresses the immediate academic challenge and enhances your child's problem-solving skills and confidence in facing future learning obstacles.

Visit a Library or Museum

When confusion surrounds a broader topic or interest, visiting a library or museum can serve as an enlightening and interactive way to seek clarity and ignite curiosity. Libraries, with their vast collections of books, periodicals, and digital resources, offer a treasure trove of information on virtually any subject, providing a quiet space for in-depth research and learning. On the other hand, museums offer a more tactile learning experience through exhibits, workshops, and guided tours, making complex topics accessible and engaging. Both settings encourage exploration and discovery in a structured yet open-ended environment, allowing your child to dive deeper into their area of confusion at their own pace. These excursions can transform the learning process into an adventure, turning abstract concepts into tangible experiences and facts.

Moreover, seeking out information together reinforces the idea that learning is a lifelong journey, not just confined to the classroom. It demonstrates your support for their interests and dedication to helping them overcome confusion, further strengthening your bond. These experiences clarify misunderstandings and foster a sense of independence and confidence in your child's ability to seek out and engage with new information.

Seek Expert Advice

When navigating more complex areas of confusion, reaching out to a teacher, counselor, or professional expert can be invaluable. These individuals bring specialized knowledge and experience, offering insights that might not be immediately apparent to parents or children. A teacher familiar with your child's learning style can provide tailored strategies to overcome educational hurdles. At the same time, a counselor might guide emotional or social confusion, offering a supportive space to explore feelings and solutions. Professional experts in specific fields can demystify complicated topics, breaking them into understandable segments. This third-party perspective can not only shed light on the issue at hand but also offer reassurance to both parent and child, demonstrating that it's okay to seek help when needed. Moreover, involving these professionals emphasizes the importance of utilizing available resources and teaches your child a valuable lesson in problem-solving and humility — that asking for help is a strength, not a weakness. This collaborative approach to resolving confusion can enhance your child's confidence in dealing with challenges, knowing they have a support system beyond the immediate family.

Role-Playing

Role-playing can be a highly effective tool to demystify interpersonal interactions if your child's confusion stems from navigating social situations. By acting out various scenarios, children can better understand social cues, appropriate responses, and how to navigate complex social dynamics. This hands-on approach allows them to experiment with different ways of reacting to situations in a safe, supportive environment, encouraging them to explore and understand the nuances of communication and social etiquette. Role-playing can specifically target areas of confusion, such as how to start a conversation, what to do when there's a disagreement, or how to interpret non-verbal cues. This practice provides clear insights into effective social strategies and helps reduce anxiety by building confidence through preparation. As children become more familiar with these simulated interactions, they can approach real-life social situations with greater ease and confidence, knowing they have the tools and experience to handle them. Furthermore, engaging in role-playing with a parent or caregiver strengthens the trust and communication in the relationship, as it demonstrates a commitment to actively supporting the child's social development and well-being.

Mind Mapping

Creating a mind map together is an innovative approach to visually organizing thoughts, questions, and information about an area of confusion, making it an excellent strategy for tackling complex topics. This collaborative process involves drawing a diagram that starts with the central subject of confusion at its core and branches out into different aspects, questions, and related ideas. By breaking down the topic into more manageable parts, a mind map can help clarify thoughts and connections that were previously muddled. It allows both parent and child to contribute their perspectives, fostering a mutual understanding and providing a clear visual representation of the problem. This method not only aids in organizing and processing information but also encourages creative thinking and problem-solving. As you and your child explore different branches of the mind map, you can identify specific areas that need further exploration, pinpoint gaps in understanding, and generate strategies for addressing them. Moreover, creating a mind map strengthens the bond between parent and child, as it requires active collaboration, listening, and sharing ideas. This engaging activity facilitates learning and comprehension and enhances communication and teamwork, making the journey from confusion to clarity a shared and supportive experience.

Encouragement and Reassurance

Feeling confused during the learning process is a natural and integral part of acquiring new knowledge and skills. This sentiment is an essential reminder for educators and parents to reassure learners, particularly children, that encountering confusion is not a sign of failure but an opportunity for growth. Educators and parents can effectively motivate and bolster their resilience by reflecting on past instances where children have successfully navigated through confusion or challenges. This approach facilitates a positive learning environment and instills confidence in learners, enabling them to embrace and overcome future challenges with a constructive perspective.

Guided Meditation or Breathing Exercises

Introducing children to simple meditation or breathing exercises can be a beneficial strategy when confusion leads to stress or anxiety, significantly aiding in clearing their minds, reducing anxiety, and enhancing focus. These techniques serve as practical tools for managing emotional responses and cognitive overload, offering a method to regain composure and concentrate more effectively on the task. By equipping children with these coping mechanisms, educators and parents can foster a more supportive learning environment that addresses the immediate challenges of stress and anxiety and promotes long-term well-being and academic success.

Create a Learning Plan

Developing a step-by-step learning plan to address confusion involves breaking down the overarching learning objective into smaller, manageable goals, making the process less intimidating and more achievable. This method starts with assessing the learner's current understanding to identify areas of confusion, followed by setting specific, measurable, attainable, relevant, and time-bound (SMART) goals. The selection of appropriate resources tailored to the learner's style and the goals at hand, alongside structured learning activities, plays a crucial role in facilitating active engagement and application of new knowledge. Monitoring progress through regular assessments and providing timely feedback allow for necessary adjustments to the plan, ensuring it remains aligned with the learner's evolving needs. Celebrating achievements along the way motivates and builds the learner's confidence in overcoming obstacles, thereby transforming confusion into a catalyst for growth and learning.

Use Analogies and Stories

Utilizing parallels from familiar stories or employing analogies is an effective strategy to demystify confusing concepts, making abstract or complex ideas more accessible and relatable. By drawing on known narratives or comparable situations, educators can bridge the gap between the learner's existing knowledge and new information, facilitating a deeper understanding. This technique not only aids in conceptualizing challenging material but also enhances retention by anchoring new ideas to familiar contexts, simplifying the learning process and making it more engaging and effective.

Patience and Persistence

Exhibiting patience and a persistent attitude in addressing confusion plays a crucial role in fostering a supportive learning environment. Educators and parents provide a comforting and encouraging message by demonstrating to children that taking the necessary time to comprehend a concept fully is acceptable. This approach alleviates the pressure to grasp new information quickly and reinforces the value of perseverance in the learning process. Encouraging patience emphasizes that understanding evolves, helping to build resilience and confidence in learners as they navigate through challenges and uncertainties in their educational journey.

These strategies are designed to address the immediate issue of confusion and foster an environment of open communication, mutual respect, and collaborative problem-solving between parents and children.

Mad:

When parents are notified that their child is feeling mad, addressing this emotion constructively is crucial for their emotional development and the parent-child bond. Here are several strategies and activities designed to navigate these feelings effectively:

Acknowledge Their Feelings

Acknowledging the legitimacy of feeling angry and providing a supportive presence for listening are pivotal first steps in addressing emotional upset. By validating these emotions, individuals are made to feel heard and understood, laying the groundwork for de-escalation. This validation acts as a crucial initial move towards calming down, serving not only to recognize the individual's emotional state but also to foster a sense of empathy and connection. It underscores the importance of emotional acknowledgment in facilitating communication and emotional regulation, ultimately aiding individuals to navigate their feelings more effectively.

Calm Conversation

After the peak intensity of anger has diminished, engaging in a calm conversation to explore the triggers behind the emotion is essential. This dialogue aims to comprehend the individual's perspective thoroughly and convey empathy. Such a discussion is pivotal as it facilitates a deeper understanding of the underlying issues and emotions, offering both parties insight into the causes of the anger. By focusing on empathy and understanding, this approach not only aids in resolving the immediate conflict but also strengthens the relationship by establishing a foundation of mutual respect and open communication. This method underscores the importance of empathy and patient listening in navigating emotional challenges and fostering positive interactions.

Teach Emotional Vocabulary

Teaching children an extensive range of emotional vocabulary is crucial in helping them articulate their feelings, which can significantly decrease frustration and misunderstandings. The ability to express emotions accurately and comprehensively provides children with a tool to convey their experiences more effectively, fostering a better understanding of their emotional state among caregivers and peers. This educational approach enhances emotional intelligence and supports emotional regulation by offering children a means to identify and communicate their feelings precisely. As a result, this method empowers children to navigate their emotional landscape more adeptly, promoting healthier emotional development and interpersonal relationships.

Cooling Down Together

Engaging in calming activities, including deep breathing exercises, taking a walk outside, or listening to calming music, effectively manages anger. By participating in these activities together, parents and educators provide immediate strategies for emotional regulation and model healthy coping mechanisms for children. This approach demonstrates practical methods for managing intense emotions, emphasizing the importance of self-regulation and the positive impact of calming activities on emotional state. It offers a dual benefit: alleviating current feelings of anger and equipping children with tools for future emotional challenges, fostering resilience and a proactive approach to emotional well-being.

Creative Expression

Encouraging children to express their feelings through creative outlets such as drawing, painting, or writing is highly beneficial in facilitating emotional expression and processing. Art serves as a powerful tool that allows children to explore and convey complex emotions tangibly and constructively. This form of expression not only aids in the articulation of feelings that might be difficult to verbalize but

75

also contributes to emotional healing and understanding. By promoting creative activities as a means for emotional expression, caregivers and educators provide children with a valuable strategy for navigating their emotional landscape, enhancing their ability to cope with and understand their feelings, thus supporting their emotional development and resilience.

Physical Activity

Physical activity can serve as an effective means for children to channel and work through their anger. Engaging in activities such as playing a sport, dancing, or participating in a family bike ride offers an outlet for releasing pent-up energy and emotions. These activities not only provide a constructive way to express feelings of frustration and anger but also promote physical health and well-being. Physical exertion can help reduce stress levels, improve mood, and foster a sense of achievement. By incorporating physical activities into their routine, children can learn to manage their emotions through positive actions, thereby developing healthier coping mechanisms for dealing with anger and other intense emotions.

Role-Playing

Using role-playing to navigate and practice handling situations that may trigger anger is a constructive approach to teaching children effective communication and emotional regulation skills. This interactive strategy allows children to experience and rehearse different scenarios in a controlled, supportive environment, allowing them to explore various responses and consequences. Through role-playing, children can gain insights into alternative ways of expressing their emotions and learn to apply problem-solving skills in conflict situations. This educational technique enhances their understanding of emotional triggers and appropriate responses and builds their confidence in managing difficult emotions. Role-playing thus serves as a valuable tool in the developmental process, equipping children with essential life skills for emotional intelligence and interpersonal communication.

Establish a 'Cool Down' Spot

Creating a designated cool-down area within the home, equipped with comforting items, is a constructive strategy for managing emotions, particularly anger. This dedicated space serves as a physical reminder and a safe haven where individuals, regardless of age, can retreat to regain composure and reflect on their emotions in a calming environment. This area can facilitate relaxation and emotional regulation by incorporating elements such as soft furnishings, stress-relief toys, art supplies, or calming music. Such a space not only underscores the importance of acknowledging and addressing emotions healthily but also promotes the development of self-regulation skills. Consequently, this approach contributes to a supportive home atmosphere where emotional well-being is prioritized and constructive emotion management is encouraged.

Set Positive Examples

Modeling positive behavior by demonstrating healthy ways to deal with anger is crucial, as children frequently learn to manage their emotions by observing adults. When parents and educators exhibit constructive responses to anger, such as verbalizing feelings calmly, engaging in problem-solving, or utilizing relaxation techniques, they provide powerful examples for children to emulate. This observational learning process is fundamental in shaping how children perceive and react to their own emotions. By witnessing adults handle anger in a controlled and healthy manner, children are more likely to adopt similar emotional regulation and expression strategies. This approach teaches children effective coping mechanisms and reinforces the importance of managing emotions in a positive and socially acceptable way, laying the foundation for their emotional intelligence and interpersonal skills.

Problem-Solving Skills

Working collaboratively to identify and address the problems that trigger anger not only resolves the immediate issue but also imparts valuable problem-solving skills to children. This cooperative approach emphasizes the significance of communication and teamwork in finding effective solutions. By engaging in this process, children learn to view challenges as opportunities for growth and development, understanding that obstacles can be overcome through constructive dialogue and mutual support. This method fosters an environment where emotional expression and practical problem-solving go hand in hand, equipping children with the necessary tools to navigate future challenges more effectively. Consequently, this strategy addresses current emotional distress and prepares children for handling similar situations in the future, promoting resilience and adaptability.

Read Books or Stories Together

Reading books that focus on emotions can significantly aid children in understanding and managing their feelings more effectively. Books that specifically address anger and outline various strategies characters use to cope with this emotion serve as valuable educational tools. Through these stories, children can identify with the characters, gaining insights into different ways of expressing and regulating anger. This method provides children with a broader perspective on emotional management and encourages empathy by allowing them to see the world through someone else's experiences. Discussing the characters' strategies for dealing with anger further reinforces the learning process, as it offers a platform for open dialogue about emotions and coping mechanisms. Hence, incorporating emotion-focused literature into a child's reading routine can enhance their emotional literacy and provide them with practical skills for navigating their feelings.

Practice Forgiveness

Teaching the importance of forgiveness towards oneself and others plays a critical role in managing emotions effectively. Children learn the value of releasing negative feelings by discussing how retaining anger can have detrimental effects. This educational approach highlights that forgiveness is an act of kindness towards others and a self-care practice that fosters emotional well-being. Understanding that holding onto anger can impact mental and physical health encourages children to embrace forgiveness, thereby reducing stress and promoting healthier relationships. Through lessons on forgiveness, children gain insights into emotional resilience and the power of moving beyond anger, equipping them with the tools to constructively handle interpersonal conflicts and emotional challenges. This fosters a positive outlook and a more compassionate approach to themselves and others.

These activities and conversations aim not only to address the immediate emotion of anger but also to build long-term skills in emotional regulation, empathy, and communication. Engaging in these practices can significantly strengthen the bond between parent and child by fostering an environment of understanding, support, and mutual respect.

Sad:

When a parent receives a notification indicating their child is feeling sad, it's important to approach the situation with sensitivity and support, fostering a closer bond through understanding and shared activities. Here are several suggestions:

Active Listening

Providing children an open, non-judgmental space to share their feelings is essential for effective emotional support. Active listening, where attention is fully given to the child without rushing to offer solutions or dismiss their emotions, conveys a deep respect for their emotional experiences. This approach reinforces the message that their feelings are valid and important, fostering a sense of security and trust. Parents and educators encourage children to express themselves openly by prioritizing understanding and empathy over immediate problem-solving, promoting emotional literacy and resilience. This supportive environment not only aids in the healthy development of emotional regulation skills but also strengthens the emotional bond between the child and the adult, establishing a foundation of mutual respect and communication.

Comfort and Reassurance

A simple gesture of comfort, such as a hug or sitting close to a child, can offer profound reassurance during times of sadness. Such actions convey a message of unconditional support and understanding, emphasizing that it is acceptable to experience and express sadness. These physical expressions of empathy and care reinforce the child's sense of security and belonging, demonstrating that they are not alone in their feelings. This level of emotional support is crucial for children as it helps them feel valued and understood and teaches them the importance of expressing emotions healthily. Consequently, through these gestures, children learn that seeking and offering support to others is a natural and positive part of emotional well-being.

Create a Feelings Journal

Encouraging children to express their emotions through writing or drawing in a personal journal gives them a valuable tool for processing their feelings. This form of expression can be particularly beneficial, as it allows children to explore and articulate their emotions privately, unfiltered. Journals serve as a safe space for self-expression and a tangible record of thoughts and feelings over time, which can be reflective and informative. Furthermore, journal entries can act as a starting point for discussions with parents or caregivers about what is bothering the child. By reviewing these entries, adults can gain insights into the child's emotional world, facilitating more meaningful and supportive conversations. This practice helps children develop emotional literacy and strengthens the communicative bond between them and their caregivers, fostering an environment of openness and trust.

Mindfulness and Relaxation

Practicing mindfulness or relaxation techniques together, such as deep breathing exercises or gentle yoga, can effectively alleviate feelings of sadness and promote a sense of calm. Engaging in these activities collaboratively provides both children and caregivers an opportunity to benefit from the calming effects of mindfulness, fostering a shared experience of tranquility and emotional regulation. Deep breathing exercises can help lower stress levels and enhance focus, while gentle yoga promotes physical relaxation and mental clarity. These practices offer immediate relief from distressing emotions and teach valuable skills for managing stress and emotional challenges in the future. By incorporating mindfulness and relaxation techniques into regular routines, families can create a nurturing environment that supports emotional well-being and resilience, encouraging healthy coping mechanisms for all family members.

Spend Quality Time Together

Engaging in activities that a child enjoys, such as a hobby, playing a game, or watching their favorite movie, plays a crucial role in showing love and attention. This approach provides an enjoyable break from routine and reinforces the child's sense of being valued and supported. Participating in these activities together demonstrates a commitment to the child's happiness and well-being, reminding them of their strong support system. Such shared experiences can strengthen the bond between children and their caregivers, fostering a positive environment where children feel secure and loved. This sense of belonging and unconditional support is essential for their emotional development and resilience, highlighting the importance of quality time in nurturing healthy relationships and emotional security.

Nature Walks

Taking a walk together in a natural setting can have a profound calming effect and significantly improve mood. The tranquil environment of nature provides a serene backdrop for meaningful conversations or shared silence, fostering a sense of connection and well-being. This activity offers an opportunity to step away from the daily stressors and immerse in the beauty and peacefulness of the natural world, which has been shown to reduce anxiety, depression, and stress. Whether through engaging dialogue or silent companionship, the experience enhances emotional bonds and supports mental health. Moreover, walking and being in nature benefits emotional and mental health and contributes to physical well-being, highlighting the multifaceted value of spending time outdoors with loved ones.

Read Together

Selecting books that address a range of emotions, including sadness, and reading them together offers a valuable opportunity for comfort and understanding. This shared activity allows for an exploration of the character's experiences and emotions, serving as a mirror for children to reflect on and articulate their feelings. Discussing the narrative and the characters' emotional journeys can help children relate to and comprehend their emotions in a more profound, more nuanced way. It also provides a safe space for open dialogue about difficult subjects, promoting emotional literacy and empathy. Furthermore, this practice reinforces the bond between the reader and child, demonstrating support and fostering a sense of security. Engaging with literature in this way not only aids in processing emotions but also enhances critical thinking and communication skills, making it a multifaceted tool for emotional and intellectual development.

Art Therapy

Encouraging children to express their emotions through art, such as painting, sculpting, or drawing, provides a therapeutic avenue for exploring and communicating feelings when words are difficult to articulate. This form of expression allows for a tangible release of emotions, offering children a creative and non-verbal way to convey their internal experiences. Artistic activities facilitate emotional processing and foster a sense of accomplishment and self-expression, contributing to a child's emotional resilience and self-esteem. Engaging in art as a form of therapy supports the development of coping strategies for managing complex emotions, making it an invaluable tool for children navigating the challenges of emotional expression. This approach underscores the importance of creative outlets in emotional health, promoting well-being and understanding through the universal language of art.

Cook or Bake Together

Preparing a favorite meal or treat together is comforting and productive, fostering a sense of connection and achievement. This shared culinary experience offers an opportunity for quality time and culminates in the rewarding enjoyment of something delicious. Engaging in cooking or baking together allows for the exchange of skills and traditions, reinforcing bonds and creating lasting memories. Moreover, making and sharing food is a nurturing gesture that communicates care and affection, contributing to a positive emotional atmosphere. This experience can be particularly beneficial during emotional distress, providing a distraction and a focus on a positive, collaborative goal. Ultimately, cooking or baking together highlights the importance of simple pleasures and the comfort of shared experiences, enhancing emotional well-being and reinforcing relationships.

Listening to Music or Dancing

Music offers a profound source of comfort and a means for expressing feelings, making it an invaluable tool for emotional support and upliftment. Creating a playlist of favorite or calming songs to listen to together provides a personalized approach to harnessing the therapeutic benefits of music, facilitating relaxation, and fostering a sense of connection. Additionally, organizing a small dance party can be an energetic and joyful activity to lift spirits, promote physical activity, and release endorphins, the body's natural mood enhancers. These musical activities not only aid in managing emotions but also encourage bonding and shared joy, highlighting the versatile role of music in enhancing emotional well-being and strengthening relationships. Engaging with music, whether through calm listening or active dancing, demonstrates the powerful impact of melody and rhythm in elevating mood and providing solace.

Plan a Future Activity

Discussing and planning a future activity or trip offers a constructive way to help a child shift focus from current sadness by fostering a sense of anticipation and excitement. This proactive approach encourages children to envision positive experiences ahead, contributing to a more optimistic outlook. Engaging in the planning process together not only serves as a distraction from immediate concerns but also strengthens the bond between the child and caregiver through shared goals and interests. Having something enjoyable to look forward to can significantly enhance a child's mood and resilience, providing them with a reminder of enjoyable moments that lie ahead. This strategy highlights the importance of hope and positive anticipation in coping with emotional challenges, promoting well-being and emotional recovery.

Encourage Helping Others

Encouraging activities centered on kindness, assisting friends and family, or engaging in volunteering can significantly enhance one's mood by fostering a sense of purpose and joy. Participating in acts of service benefits the recipients and provides the giver with a profound sense of satisfaction and well-being. This approach to emotional support underscores the concept of "helper's high," the euphoria one experiences when helping others, which can contribute to a positive self-image and emotional state. Moreover, volunteering or performing kind acts as a shared activity can strengthen social bonds and promote a sense of community and belonging. By focusing outward and contributing to the well-being of others, individuals can experience an uplift in spirits, highlighting the reciprocal nature of kindness and the impact of altruistic behaviors on emotional health.

By engaging in these activities and conversations, parents can help their children navigate feelings of sadness, offering them the tools and support needed to cope with difficult emotions while strengthening the parent-child bond through empathy, understanding, and shared experiences.

Stressed:

When a parent receives a notification that their child is experiencing stress, it's crucial to approach the situation with understanding and support, aiming to alleviate their stress while strengthening the parent-child bond. Here are several activities and conversation strategies designed for these purposes:

Open Communication

Initiating an open-ended conversation with a child about what is causing their stress provides an essential opportunity for them to share their feelings and experiences. By listening without judgment, parents and caregivers demonstrate that they take the child's emotions seriously and are committed to offering support. This active and empathetic listening approach encourages the child to express themselves freely and openly, fostering a safe and trusting environment. It underscores the importance of validating the child's feelings and experiences, which is crucial for their emotional development and well-being. Moreover, such conversations can pave the way for exploring solutions and coping strategies, reinforcing the child's sense of being supported and understood. This method highlights the role of communication in emotional support, emphasizing the value of openness and empathy in nurturing healthy relationships and promoting emotional resilience.

Relaxation Techniques

Teaching and practicing relaxation techniques together, such as deep breathing, meditation, or progressive muscle relaxation, equip children and their caregivers with effective methods for managing stress levels. When practiced regularly, these techniques can significantly reduce anxiety, improve focus, and enhance overall emotional well-being. By engaging in these activities as a shared practice, families can experience the immediate calming effects and strengthen their emotional connection by establishing a common coping mechanism for future stress. This collaborative approach to stress management fosters a supportive environment where emotional regulation skills are valued and nurtured. Additionally, it demonstrates the importance of proactive mental health care, highlighting the benefits of relaxation techniques as accessible tools for maintaining emotional balance and resilience in the face of stress.

Quality Time

Dedicating uninterrupted time to engage in enjoyable activities together, such as pursuing a hobby, taking a walk, or playing a game, is an effective stress reliever for children and their caregivers. This quality time provides a break from daily stressors and strengthens the bond between participants through shared experiences and enjoyment. Engaging in activities that both parties find enjoyable fosters a sense of joy, relaxation, and connection, contributing to a positive emotional atmosphere. This practice emphasizes valuing and making time for relationships and personal well-being amidst busy schedules. Furthermore, it highlights the role of leisure activities in promoting mental health and emotional resilience, underscoring the significance of incorporating such moments into regular routines for children and adults.

Physical Activity

Engaging in physical activity together is a potent method for reducing stress, benefiting children and adults. Exercise promotes the release of endorphins, is a natural mood lifter, improves physical health, and provides a constructive outlet for energy and tension. By selecting mutually enjoyable activities, such as biking, hiking, or playing a sport, the experience becomes more than just a routine form of exercise; it transforms into an enjoyable and bonding experience that fosters a sense of well-being and shared achievement.

94

This shared commitment to physical activity strengthens the participants' emotional bond and establishes a healthy lifestyle habit. Encouraging regular physical activity as a form of stress management underscores the importance of holistic well-being, integrating the physical, emotional, and social dimensions of health to combat stress effectively.

Creative Outlets

Encouraging participation in creative activities, including drawing, painting, music, or writing, offers a therapeutic avenue for individuals to process and reduce stress. Creative expression allows for externalizing thoughts, feelings, and experiences, providing a unique and personal way to explore and manage emotions. These activities foster a sense of accomplishment, self-discovery, and emotional release, reducing stress and enhancing mental well-being. Engaging in creative endeavors can also serve as a meditative practice, focusing the mind on the present task and providing a respite from daily stressors. Furthermore, the act of creating art or music or crafting narratives enables individuals to communicate experiences that may be difficult to articulate verbally, offering an alternative path to understanding and coping with stress. Thus, promoting creative expression as a stress management strategy highlights the importance of incorporating holistic and personal approaches to well-being, recognizing the power of creativity in fostering emotional resilience and a sense of inner peace.

Planning and Organization

If a child's stress stems from feeling overwhelmed by tasks or responsibilities, assisting them in planning and organizing their activities can be an effective strategy. Collaboratively breaking tasks into smaller, manageable steps helps mitigate the overwhelming sensation and promotes a sense of control and achievability. This process involves identifying priorities, setting realistic goals, and establishing a step-by-step approach to tackling each task. By working together to organize their responsibilities, children learn valuable time management and problem-solving skills, which are essential for reducing stress and enhancing productivity. Additionally, this shared planning process reinforces the support system available to the child, providing reassurance that they are not alone in navigating their responsibilities. Implementing this structured approach to managing tasks alleviates immediate stress and equips children with the tools to handle future challenges more effectively, promoting resilience and a proactive attitude toward problem-solving.

Healthy Lifestyle Habits

Discussing and implementing healthy lifestyle habits to combat stress is crucial to promoting overall well-being. A balanced diet, adequate sleep, and regular physical activity are foundational elements that significantly affect stress levels and emotional health. By incorporating these habits into daily routines, individuals can enhance their physical resilience against stress while improving mental clarity and emotional stability. Modeling these behaviors as a caregiver or educator demonstrates a commitment to health and a powerful influence, encouraging children to adopt similar habits. Adequate nutrition provides the energy and nutrients necessary for optimal brain function; sufficient sleep is essential for emotional regulation and cognitive performance; and regular physical activity helps release endorphins, which naturally elevate mood. By prioritizing and practicing these healthy lifestyle choices together, families and educators can create a supportive environment that underscores the importance of holistic health in managing stress and fostering a resilient, positive outlook on life.

Mindfulness Practices

Introducing mindfulness practices, such as mindful walking or eating, can significantly aid in reducing stress by fostering an awareness of the present moment. Mindful walking involves paying attention to the physical experience of walking, noticing the sensations in one's feet and the rhythm of one's breath, thereby grounding the individual in the here and now. Similarly, mindful eating encourages a focus on the sensory experience of eating, including the taste, texture, and aroma of food, which can turn a routine activity into a deliberate practice of mindfulness. These practices help to interrupt the flow of constant thoughts and worries, allowing individuals to experience a greater sense of calm and presence. Mindfulness helps manage stress by reducing rumination and anxiety and enhances overall well-being by promoting a deeper connection to one's experiences and environment. Encouraging the adoption of mindfulness practices can offer a practical and accessible approach to stress management, contributing to improved mental health and emotional resilience.

Reading and Discussion

Sharing and discussing books or articles about managing stress can enrich caregivers and children, offering insights into new methods for handling stress effectively. This practice provides a dual benefit: it introduces varied perspectives and techniques for stress management and fosters open communication about personal experiences with stress. Through engaging with and reflecting on these resources, individuals can explore and adopt strategies that resonate with their circumstances, enhancing their ability to cope with stress. Furthermore, discussing these materials can help normalize conversations about stress and mental health, reinforcing the idea that seeking improvement strategies is healthy and proactive. This approach broadens one's toolkit for managing stress and strengthens the relationship between caregivers and children by establishing a shared commitment to learning and well-being. Engaging with literature on stress management underscores the importance of continuous learning and dialogue in navigating life's challenges.

Setting Realistic Goals

Working together to set realistic goals and expectations in school, extracurricular activities, and at home is crucial in mitigating the pressure and stress of striving for perfection or over-commitment. This collaborative process ensures that the aspirations and commitments of children are aligned with their capabilities and available time, promoting a balanced approach to achievement and personal growth. Setting realistic goals involves evaluating priorities, assessing time management, and recognizing individual limits, collectively contributing to a more manageable and satisfying experience. Children are encouraged to pursue excellence without the undue stress of unrealistic expectations by focusing on achievable objectives fostering a healthier, more positive outlook on success. Furthermore, this approach emphasizes the value of self-compassion and the importance of well-being alongside accomplishment, teaching valuable life skills in goal setting, decision-making, and stress management. Engaging in this practice together reinforces the support system available to children, providing them with guidance and reassurance as they navigate their responsibilities and aspirations.

Positive Affirmations

Creating a list of positive affirmations with your child offers a tangible tool for self-support during moments of stress while simultaneously boosting their self-esteem and resilience. This collaborative activity allows children to identify and articulate their strengths, values, and aspirations, fostering a positive self-image and reinforcing their capacity to overcome challenges. Positive affirmations act as reminders of an individual's worth and capabilities, especially in moments of doubt or anxiety. By referring to these affirmations, children can shift their focus from stressors to their inner resources, promoting a sense of empowerment and emotional stability. Moreover, engaging in this activity strengthens the bond between the child and caregiver, providing a shared experience of affirmation and encouragement. This practice not only equips children with a strategy for self-compassion and positive thinking but also underlines the importance of nurturing a resilient mindset through cultivating supportive, affirming self-dialogue.

Gratitude Practice

Initiating a daily gratitude practice where individuals share something they are grateful for each day can significantly shift attention away from stressors, enhancing overall mood and perspective. This practice encourages recognizing and appreciating positive aspects of life, fostering a mindset that emphasizes abundance and positivity over lack and negativity. By reflecting on and sharing gratitude, individuals cultivate an awareness of the good in their lives, which can mitigate feelings of stress and dissatisfaction. This habit improves emotional well-being and strengthens connections between those who participate in the practice together, creating a shared space of appreciation and positivity. Additionally, focusing on gratitude has been linked to numerous benefits, including increased resilience, better sleep, and stronger relationships. Thus, incorporating a daily gratitude practice serves as a powerful tool for enhancing mental health, fostering a positive outlook, and nurturing supportive, empathetic interactions.

Stress Diary

Encouraging a child to maintain a weekly stress diary can be a highly effective method for identifying stress triggers and patterns. This practice involves recording instances of stress, noting the context, emotional responses, and coping mechanisms employed. Through this reflective process, children and their caregivers can gain valuable insights into what precipitates stress and how it manifests, facilitating a targeted approach to developing coping strategies. Analyzing the diary entries together can also foster open communication about stress and well-being, providing an opportunity to discuss and strategize ways to manage stressors more effectively. Additionally, this exercise can empower children by increasing their self-awareness and giving them a sense of control over their emotional responses. By identifying specific stress triggers and patterns, families can work together to implement changes or interventions that address the root causes of stress, leading to more effective stress management and improved overall well-being.

Learn Together

If stress management is a new endeavor for you and your child, exploring this area together through online courses or workshops focused on stress reduction techniques can be a valuable and unifying experience. Engaging in such educational opportunities allows both of you to comprehensively understand stress, its effects, and various strategies to manage it effectively. This collaborative approach to learning enhances your toolkit for dealing with stress and strengthens your relationship through shared goals and experiences. Online courses and workshops offer the flexibility to learn at your own pace and the convenience of accessing expert knowledge and practical skills from anywhere. As you and your child learn and practice new stress reduction techniques together, you can support each other in implementing these strategies into your daily lives, fostering a supportive environment for managing stress and promoting well-being. This shared journey into stress management education underscores the importance of continuous learning and mutual support in navigating life's challenges.

By employing these strategies, parents can not only help their children manage stress but also deepen their relationship, creating a foundation of trust, communication, and mutual support.

Sick:

When parents receive a notification that their child is sick, it's a time to provide extra care and attention, ensuring the child feels supported and loved. Here are activities and conversation ideas designed to comfort a sick child and strengthen the parent-child bond:

Comfort and Reassurance

Offering comfort and reassurance is a crucial first step when a child is sick, as illness can evoke feelings of fear or frustration. Acknowledging these feelings as valid and expressing your commitment to care for them can significantly alleviate their discomfort. This approach provides emotional support and strengthens the child's sense of security and trust in their caregiver. Emphasizing that you are there to help manage their symptoms and navigate the recovery process together can be immensely comforting. This form of empathy and understanding reinforces the bond between the caregiver and the child, demonstrating the importance of compassion and reassurance in fostering a nurturing and supportive environment during times of illness.

Reading Together

Choosing favorite books to read together is a soothing and energy-efficient way to spend quality time with a sick child. The activity of reading, especially when shared, can provide a comforting escape from the discomfort of illness. The familiar sound of a caregiver's voice while reading can offer a sense of comfort and normalcy, creating a calming atmosphere for the child. This practice fosters emotional bonding and supports the child's cognitive and emotional development, even during physical health challenges. Reading together requires minimal physical exertion, making it an ideal activity for rest periods. Additionally, engaging with stories can stimulate the imagination and provide a temporary diversion from any discomfort or anxiety associated with being sick. This shared experience underscores the importance of nurturing care and the power of storytelling in strengthening connections and enhancing well-being during recovery periods.

Watch a Movie or TV Show Together

Allowing your child to choose a movie or TV show to watch together can serve as a special treat and a comforting distraction, particularly when confined to bed due to illness. This activity offers relaxation and enjoyment, contributing to a more positive mood and momentarily diverting attention from discomfort. Watching something together provides entertainment and ensures that the child feels included in making decisions, fostering a sense of autonomy and importance. Moreover, this shared experience can strengthen the bond between caregiver and child, creating cherished memories even in the midst of recovery. It represents a simple yet effective way to provide emotional support and comfort, emphasizing the value of quality time and shared experiences in enhancing well-being during times of illness.

Create a Cozy Space

Creating a cozy "nest" in their room or on the couch with pillows, blankets, and their favorite stuffed animals can significantly enhance a child's comfort and sense of security during recovery. This special, comfortable space provides physical warmth and comfort and offers emotional support, making the recovery period feel more bearable and less daunting. Incorporating elements that the child loves and finds comforting reinforces their feeling of safety and care. This personalized recovery area can serve as a soothing sanctuary where the child can rest, read, watch movies, or engage in other low-energy activities. Additionally, setting up this cozy space with the child can further convey your care and dedication to their well-being, strengthening the emotional connection and reassuring them that they are not alone in their recovery journey. This thoughtful gesture underscores the importance of a nurturing environment in facilitating a child's recovery and overall well-being.

Listen to Audiobooks or Music

If your child is not in the mood for watching TV or reading, listening to audiobooks or soothing music presents a valuable alternative for relaxation and entertainment. This option allows the child to rest their eyes and still engage with compelling stories or enjoy calming melodies, significantly contributing to a peaceful environment conducive to recovery. Choosing audiobooks with stories they enjoy or music that soothes them can make the experience personalized and more enjoyable, offering a sense of normalcy and pleasure even when they're feeling unwell. This form of entertainment requires minimal effort on the child's part but can still significantly positively impact their mood and overall sense of well-being. Additionally, listening together can be a bonding experience, offering comfort and connection without the need for physical activity, further demonstrating your support and care during their recovery period.

Simple Crafts or Coloring

Engaging in simple crafts or coloring offers a gentle and creative distraction for a child who is feeling unwell, catering to their fluctuating energy levels. Selecting relaxing and not overly demanding activities can provide a therapeutic outlet, allowing the child to express themselves creatively without exerting too much energy. Crafts and coloring can be particularly beneficial as they focus the mind on the task, reducing stress and diverting attention from discomfort. These activities also contribute to a sense of accomplishment and normalcy, enhancing the child's mood and promoting a more positive outlook during recovery. Furthermore, participating in these activities can strengthen the caregiver-child bond, providing an opportunity for shared experiences and emotional support. Carefully choosing crafts or coloring projects that align with the child's interests and energy level ensures that the activities are enjoyable and conducive to the child's well-being and recovery.

Hydration and Nutrition

Discussing the importance of staying hydrated and offering favorite soups or easy-to-eat nutritious meals can significantly aid a child's recovery process. Hydration plays a key role in healing, helping to ensure that the body functions properly and remains resilient. Soups can be particularly soothing, offering hydration and nutrition in an easily digestible form, especially beneficial if the child has a reduced appetite or difficulty eating solid foods.

Making meal and drink choices more engaging by allowing the child to select from healthy options gives them a sense of autonomy and involvement in their care, potentially increasing their willingness to eat or drink. This approach meets their nutritional needs and boosts their spirits by incorporating elements of normal daily life into the recovery process. Preparing and presenting meals together can also be a comforting and bonding activity, reinforcing the caregiver's support and care. By focusing on hydration and nutrition through preferred and appealing options, caregivers can effectively support the child's recovery, emphasizing the importance of healthy eating and drinking habits in a manner that is both caring and engaging.

Share Stories

Sharing personal stories from your childhood about times when you were sick can significantly foster a sense of empathy and connection with your child. Relating experiences of how you felt, what helped you recover, and who looked after you during those times humanizes the experience of illness for the child and offers comfort and reassurance. It demonstrates that they are not alone in their feelings and that needing care and comfort when unwell is normal. Such stories can also provide practical insights into coping mechanisms or remedies that might still be relevant. Moreover, hearing about how others have navigated similar challenges can be empowering and encouraging for a child. This exchange of personal experiences enhances the bond between caregiver and child, creating a shared understanding and deepening emotional support during times of vulnerability. It highlights the universality of care and compassion, reinforcing that sickness is a shared human experience navigated with the help of loved ones.

Gentle Massage or Back Rub

Offering a gentle massage or back rub can provide significant physical comfort to a child who is not feeling well, serving as a soothing and nurturing form of care. This type of physical touch helps to relax tense muscles, alleviate discomfort, and convey a strong sense of safety, love, and attention from the caregiver. Providing gentle physical comfort can promote relaxation and potentially ease symptoms, such as headaches or general body aches associated with illness. Additionally, the close, caring interaction involved in a massage or back rub can strengthen the emotional bond between the caregiver and child, reinforcing the child's sense of being cared for and supported during their recovery. This comfort method highlights the importance of compassionate, tactile support in enhancing a child's well-being and can effectively complement other care strategies during times of illness.

Discussing Health and Wellness

Using the time during a child's illness as an opportunity to discuss the importance of health, how the body fights off illness, and the significance of rest and proper care can be both educational and reassuring. Tailoring the conversation to be age-appropriate ensures that the child can understand and engage with the information. For younger children, simple explanations and analogies related to soldiers (immune cells) fighting off invaders (viruses and bacteria) can make the immune system concept tangible and less intimidating. For older children, more detailed discussions about how the body's defenses work, the role of vaccines in aiding these defenses, and the importance of nutrition and hydration in recovery can foster a deeper understanding and appreciation of their bodies' capabilities.

Explaining the need for rest and proper care as essential components of recovery emphasizes the body's requirements for healing and the active role the child can play in their health. Such conversations educate the child about their health and well-being and empower them with the knowledge to take proactive steps towards recovery and future illness prevention. This approach addresses immediate health concerns and lays the groundwork for lifelong healthy habits and a positive relationship with well-being.

Plan for When They're Better

Discussing activities or outings to enjoy together once the child feels better can significantly lift their spirits by providing them with something positive to anticipate. Planning future fun activities—whether it's a visit to a favorite park, a movie day, a trip to the zoo, or even a simple ice cream outing—can offer a sense of excitement and normalcy amidst the discomfort of being ill. This progressive approach not only motivates the child to focus on recovery but also strengthens the emotional bond between the child and caregiver, highlighting the joy of shared experiences. By involving the child in choosing these activities, you further validate their feelings and preferences, reinforcing their sense of autonomy and importance in decision-making. This strategy underscores the power of positive anticipation in enhancing mood and the therapeutic value of looking forward to shared moments of happiness and connection.

Quiet Time Together

Being present with a child who is not feeling well can convey a profound sense of safety and care, offering significant comfort during times of illness. The act of sitting quietly together, without the need for conversation or activities, can be incredibly reassuring for a child. This quiet companionship communicates that they are not alone and that their well-being is a priority, providing a stable and comforting presence that can ease discomfort or anxiety. The caregiver's presence alone can be a powerful form of emotional support, underscoring the importance of non-verbal communication in conveying love and concern. This approach emphasizes the value of emotional availability and the impact of physical presence in nurturing a child's sense of security and belonging, highlighting that sometimes, the simplest forms of support are the most meaningful.

These activities and conversations can help a sick child feel loved and cared for, while also providing opportunities for parents to nurture and strengthen their bond during a challenging time.

Tired:

When a child feels tired, it's an opportunity for parents to engage in gentle and nurturing activities that not only respect the child's need for rest but also strengthen the parent-child bond. Here are several ideas:

Quiet Time Together

Sitting quietly with your child under a cozy blanket, offering your presence as a comforting support, can be an incredibly soothing experience for them. This form of quiet companionship is a powerful gesture of care and reassurance, emphasizing that they are not alone and that their comfort is of utmost importance. Being together in silence allows for a peaceful exchange of support and love without needing words. This can be especially comforting during times of illness or distress, as the physical presence of a caregiver can provide a sense of security and calm. Such moments of silent solidarity can strengthen the bond between caregiver and child, underscoring the profound impact of non-verbal communication and the simple yet significant power of just being there for one another. This approach highlights the importance of emotional presence and the comforting reassurance it brings, offering a gentle reminder of the healing power of quiet, shared moments.

Reading Aloud

Choosing your favorite books to read to your child during times of illness or fatigue can turn a challenging period into a memorable and comforting experience. The sound of a caregiver's voice while reading can provide significant emotional comfort, enveloping the child in a familiar and soothing auditory embrace. This activity allows for meaningful connection without requiring the child to engage fully, which is particularly beneficial if they are too tired or unwell to participate actively. Reading aloud offers a distraction from discomfort, a way to pass the time pleasantly, and an opportunity to continue learning and experiencing new stories or revisiting beloved tales. Additionally, this practice nurtures a love for reading and storytelling, enriching the child's cognitive and emotional development. The act of reading to a child in this way underscores the importance of nurturing care, demonstrating that moments of illness can also be opportunities for closeness, comfort, and shared joy.

Gentle Massage or Back Rub

Offering a gentle back rub or foot massage provides a form of physical comfort that can be profoundly relaxing for a tired child, helping them to unwind and feel nurtured. This tactile expression of care can significantly alleviate physical tension and emotional stress, promoting a sense of well-being and safety. The soothing touch of a back rub or foot massage not only aids in relaxation but also communicates love and support directly, enhancing the child's sense of being cared for. Such acts of kindness can strengthen the emotional bond between the caregiver and the child, reinforcing a nurturing relationship. Moreover, the relaxation induced by gentle massage can improve the child's quality of sleep, further contributing to their recovery and overall health. This method of providing comfort highlights the importance of attentive care and the positive impact of physical touch in conveying affection and fostering a calming, supportive environment.

Listen to Soft Music or Audiobooks

Playing soft music or an audiobook effectively creates a relaxing atmosphere for a child needing rest or feeling unwell. Selecting soothing tunes or a story they enjoy can provide a gentle distraction, easing stress and creating a sense of calm. This activity is especially beneficial as it requires minimal energy from the child yet offers significant emotional and mental comfort. Music has the power to soothe and heal, reducing anxiety and promoting relaxation, while audiobooks can transport the listener to another world, offering respite from discomfort and boredom. This approach supports the child's need for rest and recovery and keeps their mind engaged in a peaceful, enjoyable way. Incorporating soft music or audiobooks into the child's relaxation routine can enhance their well-being, demonstrating the caregiver's thoughtful consideration for their comfort and enjoyment even in moments of low energy.

Discuss the Day

Having a calm conversation about their day, focusing on listening to their experiences and feelings, can significantly aid a child in processing the events of their day and transitioning into a state of rest. This reflective dialogue provides an opportunity for the child to express themselves freely, share any concerns or highlights, and feel heard and valued. Such conversations can be therapeutic, allowing the child to unpack their thoughts and emotions, which might otherwise go unaddressed. Caregivers reinforce the child's sense of security and trust by actively listening and engaging with empathy, demonstrating that their experiences and feelings matter. This practice fosters emotional well-being and strengthens the bond between the caregiver and the child, establishing a routine of open communication and mutual support. This gentle end-of-day reflection can ease the transition into sleep, promoting a peaceful and restorative rest and highlighting the importance of emotional processing as part of the bedtime routine.

Mindfulness or Relaxation Exercises

Practicing simple mindfulness or relaxation exercises together, such as deep breathing or guided imagery, can effectively calm a busy mind and facilitate a state of rest. These techniques focus on slowing down the breath and visualizing peaceful scenes, which can significantly reduce stress levels and quiet mental chatter. Engaging in these activities together provides a shared experience of relaxation, reinforcing the caregiver's role in supporting the child's emotional well-being. Deep breathing exercises encourage a physiological shift that promotes relaxation by increasing the oxygen supply to the brain and stimulating the parasympathetic nervous system, which has a calming effect. Guided imagery, on the other hand, helps the child escape to a serene environment, further aiding in relaxation and stress reduction. By incorporating these practices into the child's routine, especially before bedtime, caregivers can help the child develop effective coping mechanisms for managing stress and preparing their mind and body for rest, highlighting the importance of mindfulness and relaxation in promoting overall well-being and restful sleep.

Create a Bedtime Routine Together

If a child consistently experiences tiredness, collaboratively establishing a soothing bedtime routine can be beneficial. This routine might include taking a warm bath, reading a story, or spending quiet time together. These activities create a calming, predictable pattern that cues the body when it's time to transition to sleep. The consistency of such a routine is critical, as it helps regulate the child's internal clock and eases the shift from wakefulness to sleepiness, enhancing the quality and ease of falling asleep. A warm bath can relax the muscles and lower the body's temperature afterward, which signals the body it's time to sleep. Reading a story provides a quiet, engaging activity and fosters a sense of closeness and security. Quiet time together can offer a peaceful moment for winding down and reflecting on the day. By tailoring the bedtime routine to include activities the child finds most relaxing, caregivers can effectively support the child's need for rest, demonstrating the importance of structure and relaxation in promoting healthy sleep habits and overall well-being.

Prepare a Warm Drink

Preparing a warm, non-caffeinated drink like milk or herbal tea to share can create a comforting and serene moment, potentially evolving into a cherished nightly routine. This simple act offers physical warmth and an opportunity for emotional connection, providing a sense of calm and closeness. Warm beverages can have a soothing effect on the body, facilitating relaxation and making it easier to transition into a restful state before bed. Herbal teas, in particular, can offer various calming properties, while warm milk has long been associated with inducing sleepiness. Sharing this quiet time allows for a few moments of reflection and connection, free from the distractions of daily life. By incorporating this into the evening routine, caregivers can reinforce the importance of slowing down and nurturing relationships, establishing a ritual that underscores the value of care, comfort, and quality time together. This practice not only aids in winding down for the night but also strengthens bonds, making it a meaningful addition to bedtime preparations.

Plan a Restful Day

Planning a restful day with no obligations can effectively respond to consistent tiredness in a child, allowing them to recharge. This day should include relaxing activities the child enjoys, whether reading, drawing, watching favorite movies, or simply lounging in a comfortable space. The key is to create an environment free from the usual demands and pressures, allowing the child to engage in activities at their own pace and according to their interests. Such a day can serve as a valuable break, offering physical rest and mental and emotional relaxation. By prioritizing rest and relaxation in this intentional manner, caregivers demonstrate the importance of listening to one's body and taking proactive steps to maintain well-being. This approach also teaches the child about the value of self-care and the importance of recovering from the cumulative effects of daily stresses. A restful day spent together can strengthen the bond between caregiver and child, reinforcing that taking care of one's health is a priority and that it's okay to take a step back and rest when needed.

Reflect on Sleep Hygiene

Discussing the importance of good sleep hygiene with a child in an age-appropriate manner involves explaining how certain habits and the sleep environment can significantly impact the quality of their sleep. For younger children, this can be framed around the concept of creating a cozy and comfortable "nest" for sleep, emphasizing the need to put "busy" toys or electronics to "sleep" in another room to help their minds relax. You might use simple stories or analogies to illustrate how the body and brain need quiet time to grow strong and healthy.

For older children, the conversation can be more direct, discussing how the light from screens can trick their brains into thinking it's still daytime, making it harder to fall asleep. You can talk about the science of sleep in simple terms, like how sleep is food for the brain, helping them learn, grow, and feel happy.

Together, brainstorm ways to improve sleep, such as creating a bedtime routine that includes winding down with a book instead of a screen, making the bedroom a comfortable and quiet place for sleep, or setting a consistent bedtime. Encourage them to contribute ideas and express what makes them feel most relaxed at bedtime. This collaborative approach educates the child on the importance of sleep and empowers them to take an active role in improving their sleep habits. Highlighting the connection between their actions and how they feel the next day reinforces the importance of good sleep hygiene in a way that is meaningful and motivating for them.

Express Understanding and Empathy

Letting your child know that feeling tired is a normal part of life and something everyone experiences can be very reassuring for them. Sharing your experiences with tiredness and the strategies you use to cope with it helps normalize these feelings, making the child feel understood and less isolated. Discussing how you recognize signs of tiredness in yourself, the importance of listening to your body's needs, and taking actions such as resting, adjusting your activities, or ensuring you get a good night's sleep can provide practical examples for your child to emulate. This conversation can also be an opportunity to highlight the importance of self-care and the various ways to manage tiredness, including relaxation techniques, healthy eating, and physical activity. By opening up about your experiences, you offer your child valuable coping strategies and strengthen your connection with them through shared vulnerabilities and solutions. This approach underscores the message that it's okay to take a break and look after oneself, fostering an environment of understanding and support.

Prioritize Rest

Emphasizing the importance of listening to one's body and resting when needed is crucial for a child's understanding of self-care and health management. Teaching children to recognize and respond to their body's signals for rest encourages them to prioritize their health and well-being. It's beneficial to make it clear that their health is a top priority and that taking time to rest is acceptable and necessary for recovery and maintaining good health. By fostering an environment where health and well-being are valued, children learn to make informed decisions about their self-care. This self-awareness and health management lesson is instrumental in developing lifelong habits prioritizing well-being. Reinforcing this message also demonstrates care and support for the child's overall health, showing them that their feelings and needs are important and respected.

These activities and conversations are designed to support a tired child in a way that respects their need for rest while also deepening the parent-child connection through care, understanding, and shared quiet moments.

Depressed:

When parents are alerted that their child might be experiencing depression, it's crucial to approach the situation with sensitivity, support, and a willingness to understand their feelings deeply. The following are activities and conversations aimed at supporting a child through such a time while also working to strengthen the bond between parent and child:

Open and Supportive Conversations

Initiating gentle conversations and encouraging your child to express their feelings and thoughts is pivotal in fostering an environment where they feel safe and understood. By showing unconditional support and listening without judgment, you communicate to your child that their emotions and perspectives are valid and important. This approach helps build trust and strengthens the emotional bond between you and your child. Children need to know they have a safe space to share their experiences, worries, and joys. Encouraging open dialogue about feelings and thoughts allows children to develop healthy emotional expression and coping skills. Demonstrating empathy and understanding in these conversations reassures the child of your support, helping them navigate their emotions more confidently. Active and compassionate listening is a cornerstone of nurturing a positive, supportive relationship, ensuring the child feels valued and heard.

Quality Time Together

Spending quality time together engaging in activities your child enjoys or finds comforting is crucial in nurturing your relationship and supporting their emotional well-being, even if these activities are low-energy. Whether it's watching their favorite movie, taking a quiet walk, or simply sitting together in nature, these moments offer a shared experience of relaxation and joy. The simplicity of these activities allows for a focus on being together rather than on the activity itself, emphasizing the value of your presence and attention. Such experiences can be particularly comforting for a child, providing them with a sense of security and belonging. Engaging in activities your child loves or finds soothing shows that you value their interests and well-being, reinforcing their importance to you. This dedicated time together strengthens your bond and communicates your commitment to supporting their happiness and emotional health, highlighting the significance of quality time in building strong, supportive relationships.

Encourage Expressive Outlets

Encouraging your child to express themselves through creative outlets such as art, music, writing, or dance is invaluable for their emotional development and well-being. Creative expression offers a powerful avenue for children to explore and convey their feelings in a constructive and often therapeutic manner. These activities provide a safe space for children to navigate complex emotions, allowing for self-discovery and emotional release. Engaging in creative pursuits can also enhance a child's self-esteem and confidence as they see their thoughts and feelings take shape in tangible forms. Whether it's through the strokes of a paintbrush, the melody of an instrument, the structure of a story, or the movement of dance, children learn to communicate in ways that words alone may not suffice. This form of expression not only aids in processing emotions but also fosters a sense of accomplishment and identity. By supporting and encouraging these creative endeavors, caregivers can help children develop a deeper understanding of themselves and their emotions, demonstrating the importance of creativity as a tool for emotional expression and resilience.

Physical Activity

Engaging in gentle physical activities together, like walking, yoga, or stretching, improves mood and facilitates bonding. These activities stimulate the release of endorphins, often referred to as the body's natural mood elevators, which can help to alleviate stress and enhance overall well-being. Gentle exercise is particularly beneficial as it can be adapted to suit all ages and fitness levels, ensuring it's an inclusive activity for the whole family. By participating in these activities together, you create shared experiences that strengthen your relationship, providing quality time that encourages communication and mutual support. Furthermore, incorporating regular physical activity into your routine sets a positive example for maintaining a healthy lifestyle, highlighting the importance of caring for both physical and mental health. This approach supports the child's well-being and reinforces the bond between caregiver and child, making it a valuable practice for fostering emotional closeness and family unity.

Mindfulness and Relaxation

Practicing mindfulness or relaxation techniques together, such as meditation or deep breathing exercises, can significantly contribute to alleviating symptoms of depression and promoting a sense of calm. These practices encourage a focus on the present moment, helping to reduce overwhelming feelings and fostering an environment of peace and stillness. Engaging in these activities as a shared experience can enhance the sense of connection and support, making it easier to navigate complex emotions together. Mindfulness and deep breathing exercises can lower stress levels, improve emotional regulation, and increase self-awareness, benefiting both the individual and the relationship. By incorporating these techniques into your routine, you demonstrate the importance of mental health maintenance and provide practical tools for managing stress and depression. This shared commitment to well-being not only aids in the management of depressive symptoms but also strengthens the bond through a mutual understanding of the value of mental health.

Routine and Structure

Helping your child establish a routine that includes regular sleep, meals, and physical activity can provide them with stability and security. A structured daily routine helps to set expectations and establish norms, reducing uncertainty and anxiety by offering predictability in their day-to-day life. Regular sleep patterns are essential for mental and physical health, supporting cognitive function, mood regulation, and overall well-being. Consistent meal times ensure proper nutrition and offer opportunities for family bonding and communication. Including physical activity in the routine contributes to physical health, enhances mood by releasing endorphins, and can be a constructive outlet for stress and excess energy. Establishing such a routine fosters a healthy lifestyle and instills habits supporting emotional and physical health. By actively participating in creating and maintaining this routine, caregivers provide support and guidance, demonstrating the importance of self-care and the benefits of structure in achieving a balanced, healthy life.

Positive Reinforcement

Acknowledging your child's efforts and accomplishments, regardless of their scale, is pivotal in boosting their self-esteem and motivating continued engagement in activities. Positive reinforcement celebrates the process of learning and growing, emphasizing the value of effort and perseverance. This approach nurtures a positive self-image and encourages children to embrace challenges confidently. Recognizing big and small achievements signals to your child that their actions and contributions are valued and important. Such validation fosters a supportive environment where children feel seen and appreciated, which is instrumental in developing a healthy sense of self-worth. Moreover, this practice of positive reinforcement can enhance a child's motivation to pursue interests and tackle new challenges, reinforcing the importance of effort and resilience. By consistently applying positive reinforcement, caregivers can significantly influence their child's emotional and developmental growth, laying a foundation for lifelong learning and self-esteem.

Connect with Nature

Spending time together in natural settings can significantly enhance emotional well-being and calm and improve mood. Nature provides a serene and beautiful backdrop for activities, fostering relaxation and a sense of peace. The natural environment encourages mindfulness and present-moment awareness, allowing deeper conversation and reflection. This connection with nature can reduce feelings of stress and anxiety, promoting mental health and providing a refreshing break from the hustle and bustle of daily life. Engaging in outdoor activities like walking, hiking, or simply sitting and observing the natural surroundings can strengthen bonds by creating shared experiences and memories. Furthermore, exposure to natural light and fresh air benefits physical health, enhancing the overall experience. By prioritizing time spent in nature, families can enjoy a unique and enriching environment that nurtures individual and collective well-being, highlighting the therapeutic benefits of the natural world.

Shared Learning

Learning about depression together, including its symptoms, causes, and treatments, can play a crucial role in demystifying the condition and facilitating open discussions about mental health. This educational approach can help dispel myths and misconceptions about depression, making it a less daunting topic to address. By gaining a shared understanding, families can foster a supportive environment where members feel safe to express their feelings and seek help without fear of judgment or stigma. Understanding depression together encourages empathy, awareness, and a proactive stance toward mental health, emphasizing the importance of compassion and informed support. Additionally, this collective learning process can significantly reduce feelings of isolation for those experiencing depression, as it highlights the condition's commonality and the availability of effective treatments. Educating oneself and others about depression is a vital step in promoting mental health awareness, reducing stigma, and encouraging a supportive community where individuals feel empowered to discuss and address their mental health needs.

Professional Support

Encouraging the pursuit of help from a mental health professional and offering support throughout the process is critical in navigating mental health challenges effectively. Offering assistance in finding a therapist, attending appointments together when appropriate, or simply being available to discuss their feelings about therapy can significantly ease the apprehension associated with seeking mental health care. This support underscores the importance of addressing mental health needs and reinforces that seeking help is a strength, not a weakness. By actively participating in the process, caregivers demonstrate a commitment to the well-being of their loved ones, creating a foundation of trust and openness. This approach facilitates access to professional help and promotes a positive perspective towards therapy and mental health care. Providing such support can play a vital role in the individual's journey toward healing and recovery, emphasizing the value of compassionate assistance and the significance of mental health in overall well-being.

Plan Future Activities

Planning future activities or outings that your child can look forward to is a beneficial strategy for lifting spirits and instilling a sense of hope. Anticipation of enjoyable events can serve as a positive focus, offering light during challenging times. Whether it's a simple family outing, visiting a favorite place, or participating in an activity they love, having these events on the horizon can motivate and encourage your child. This strategic approach provides immediate joy in the planning process and reinforces the concept that there are enjoyable moments to be had in the future. It's an effective way to demonstrate the cyclic nature of life—that periods of difficulty are often followed by times of joy. Involving your child in the planning process can enhance their sense of control and involvement, making the anticipated activity even more meaningful. This practice of looking forward to positive experiences underscores the importance of hope and optimism in maintaining mental and emotional well-being.

Healthy Lifestyle Choices

Discussing and implementing healthy lifestyle choices, focusing on nutritious eating, and ensuring adequate sleep can significantly impact mood and overall well-being. Engaging in these discussions emphasizes the importance of taking care of one's body as a foundation for mental health. Nutritious eating provides the body with the necessary vitamins and minerals to function optimally, supporting brain health and emotional regulation. Adequate sleep is crucial for recovery, cognitive function, and emotional resilience, affecting one's ability to manage stress and maintain a positive mood.

By making these lifestyle choices a shared endeavor, families can foster an environment of mutual support and accountability, making it easier to adopt and maintain these healthy habits. This approach benefits individual family members and strengthens family bonds through collective participation in healthy behaviors. Implementing changes together, such as preparing healthy meals or establishing a regular sleep routine, demonstrates a commitment to each other's health and well-being, highlighting the interconnectedness of physical and mental well-being. This collaborative effort reinforces the idea that small, consistent lifestyle changes can profoundly impact one's mood and overall quality of life.

Family Support System

Creating a supportive family environment where feelings can be openly discussed, and everyone supports each other is essential in fostering emotional well-being and resilience. Such an environment encourages all family members to express their thoughts and emotions without fear of judgment, reinforcing the idea that it's okay to talk about one's feelings, regardless of their nature. Open communication within the family can significantly reduce feelings of isolation and increase your child's sense of belonging and support.

This supportive atmosphere is cultivated through regular family discussions, active listening, and showing empathy and understanding towards each other's experiences. Encouraging expressions of support and solidarity, recognizing each other's efforts and accomplishments, and navigating challenges together strengthen family bonds and promote a healthy, communicative relationship among all members. This approach helps your child feel less alone and models positive interpersonal skills and emotional intelligence. A family environment that prioritizes open communication and mutual support lays the groundwork for a secure, nurturing space where every member can thrive emotionally and feel empowered to face life's challenges with confidence.

Gratitude Practice

Starting a daily practice of sharing things you're each grateful for can profoundly impact the family's overall mood and perspective. This practice encourages focusing on life's positive aspects, helping shift attention away from negative thoughts and feelings. By taking time each day to reflect on and express gratitude, family members can cultivate a more optimistic outlook, recognizing the value and abundance in their lives, even in small, everyday moments.

This habit of gratitude can strengthen family bonds, as sharing these moments opens a window into each other's values and appreciations, fostering deeper connections and understanding. It also serves as a powerful reminder of the support and love present within the family, offering a sense of stability and reassurance.

Moreover, research has shown that gratitude is associated with increased happiness, reduced stress, and an overall improvement in well-being. Integrating this practice into daily life benefits individual family members and contributes to a more positive and supportive family environment. Encouraging everyone to participate can turn gratitude sharing into a cherished part of the day, reinforcing positive interactions and the importance of acknowledging and appreciating life's blessings.

Engaging in these activities and conversations can provide critical support for a child experiencing depression, ensuring they feel loved, understood, and not alone. It's important to approach the situation with empathy, patience, and a willingness to seek professional help when necessary.

Made in the USA
Las Vegas, NV
20 February 2025